Peacebuilding Toolkit for Educators

Peacebuilding Toolkit for Educators
Middle School Lessons

Alison Milofsky, editor

with contributions by

Kristina Berdan

Sarah Bever

Danielle Goldberg

Nora Gordon

Illana Lancaster

Adriana Murphy

Terese Trebilcock

UNITED STATES INSTITUTE OF PEACE PRESS
Washington, D.C.

The views expressed in this book are those of the authors alone. They do not necessarily reflect views of the United States Institute of Peace.

UNITED STATES INSTITUTE OF PEACE
2301 Constitution Avenue, NW
Washington, DC 20037
www.usip.org

First published 2011. Second printing 2012

Printed in the United States of America

The paper used in this publication meets the minimum requirements of American National Standards for Information Science—Permanence of Paper for Printed Library Materials, ANSI Z39.48-1984.

Library of Congress Cataloging-in-Publication Data

Peacebuilding toolkit for educators: middle school lessons / Alison Milofsky, editor; with contributions by Kristina Berdan . . . [et al.].
   p. cm.
  ISBN 978-1-60127-105-1 (alk. paper)
   1. Peace-building—Study and teaching (Middle school)   2. Conflict management—Study and teaching (Middle school)   3. Peace-building—Study and teaching (Middle school)—Activity programs.   4. Conflict management—Study and teaching (Middle school)—Activity programs.   I. Milofsky, Alison.   II. Berdan, Kristina.
  JZ5534.P44 2011
  303.6'60712—dc23
                                 2011029995

PEACEBUILDING TOOLKIT FOR EDUCATORS

Introduction 7

About the Peacebuilding Toolkit for Educators 7

To the Educator: A Letter of Welcome 7

Organizing Principles: What are the assumptions on which the toolkit is based? 8

Audience: Who is the toolkit's intended audience? *8*

Using the Toolkit: What do you need to know before you start? *8*

Standards: How do the lessons align with standards? *9*

Assessment: How do you assess lessons on peacebuilding and conflict? *10*

Guidelines for Teaching about Global Peacebuilding 10

Why teach global peacebuilding? *10*

Considerations for teaching about global peacebuilding *10*

About USIP 13

Institute Activities *13*

About USIP's Global Peacebuilding Center *13*

Section 1: Conflict is an inherent part of the human condition. 15

Lesson 1.1 Defining Conflict (Parts 1 and 2) 17

Lesson 1.2 Perspectives on Peace (Parts 1 and 2) 27

Section 2: Violent conflict can be prevented. 37

Lesson 2.1 Observing Conflict 39

Lesson 2.2 Identifying Conflict Styles 45

Lesson 2.3 Practicing Conflict Analysis 51

Lesson 2.4A Responding to Conflict: Nonverbal Communication 59

Lesson 2.4B Responding to Conflict: Active Listening 63

Lesson 2.4C Responding to Conflict: Negotiation—Identifying Wants and Needs ... 69

Lesson 2.4D Responding to Conflict: Negotiation Role-play 77

Lesson 2.4E Responding to Conflict: Mediation 85

Section 3: There are many ways to be a peacebuilder. 93

Lesson 3.1 Characteristics of Peacebuilders 95

Lesson 3.2 Peacebuilders in Action 99

Lesson 3.3 Organizations Working for Peace *105*

Lesson 3.4 Making a Difference: Becoming a Peacebuilder *111*

Lesson 3.5 Taking a Step Toward Peacebuilding *117*

Appendix

Participation Rubric *119*

Feedback Form *121*

About the Contributors *123*

INTRODUCTION

About the Peacebuilding Toolkit for Educators

To the Educator: A Letter of Welcome

The United States Institute of Peace (USIP) is an independent, nonpartisan institution established by Congress to increase the nation's capacity to manage international conflict without violence. We do this, in part, by providing others with the knowledge, skills, and resources to engage effectively in conflict management. Educating the public, and particularly younger audiences, about the challenges and importance of peacebuilding is part of our core mission.

This *Peacebuilding Toolkit for Educators* is designed to support the work of educators as peacebuilders. We believe that young people have tremendous capacity, as individuals and as a community, to learn about and contribute to international conflict management, and that educators can channel students' energy and enthusiasm in positive ways. We also wish to provide you with guidance and materials about the complex nature of peacebuilding. We have created this toolkit and dedicated a section on our Global Peacebuilding Center website to providing materials and lessons for middle school and high school students, interactive exercises, and a discussion forum where you can gain input on the difficult questions that arise in your classroom.

The focus of this toolkit is on peacebuilding because we know that peacebuilding must be developed, fostered, and supported. Our goal is to help in the development of young people as peacebuilders and to raise the visibility of positive examples of nonviolent conflict management.

The purpose of this toolkit is not to tell students what to think; rather, we want to encourage students to think critically about the world around them and their place in it. It is our belief that the skills of peacebuilding presented in this toolkit are applicable at multiple levels. The tools that peer mediators use in middle school and high school conflict resolution programs are in many ways similar to some of the tools used by diplomats and heads of state in international peace negotiations. While international conflicts are often far more complex, the core skills of active listening, relationship building, and working cooperatively to find mutually agreeable solutions among parties apply at all levels.

As you explore this toolkit and experiment with the lessons in your classroom, please consider providing us with feedback via the survey at the end of the toolkit or online. As a community of educators, we can continue to develop and improve upon our lessons based on your practical experience in the classroom.

Organizing Principles: What are the assumptions on which the toolkit is based?

This toolkit is organized around a few basic ideas within the field of international conflict management.

1. **Conflict is an inherent part of the human condition.**
   Conflict is natural, and as such, it cannot be eliminated from society. Conflict is a normal part of everyday life and it is part of living in a thriving, pluralistic democracy. What makes a democratic society successful is its ability to deal with conflict, to allow and manage disagreement and dissent among people.

2. **Violent conflict can be prevented.**
   Conflict becomes problematic when it escalates to violence. But violent conflict can be prevented. We can teach our students to assert their opinion while being respectful and open to the ideas of others; to listen with care and attentiveness; and to act responsibly when faced with conflict. Conflict need not cross the line to violence. Whether on a personal or an international level, managing conflict is possible when parties in conflict with one another use peacebuilding tools to manage their disagreement.

3. **There are many ways to be a peacebuilder.**
   Peacebuilding is based on knowledge, skills, and attitudes that can be learned. As such, everyone can be a peacebuilder. But it is a conscious choice that involves making decisions and taking actions that require effort.

Audience: Who is the toolkit's intended audience?

The toolkit is designed for a general audience of students in grades 6–8. The content can be modified for older students and some of the content can be modified for younger students. Engaging young audiences in conversations about peace and conflict is important. It is our hope that young students will engage in these topics and continue to reflect on them as they progress through high school and move into the world. The lessons have been developed with great detail to be useful for educators who are new to the methods employed that engage students in experiential learning and critical thinking. The lessons are intended for traditional and alternative education settings.

Using the Toolkit: What do you need to know before you start?

Overview of Lessons

The lessons in the toolkit are interactive and encourage students to work collaboratively to understand concepts and solve problems. The lessons are designed to be detailed enough for a new teacher or a teacher unfamiliar with interactive or experiential methods to pick them up and use them as intended. The middle school lessons include teacher direction, guided practice, and independent practice. The lessons are structured this way to meet the developmental needs of middle school students. At the middle school level, students benefit from a personal connection in order to develop context for concepts. By modeling and then providing students with opportunities to experiment with the content on their own, teachers can assess who understands the material and who does not. Students in middle school are learning to take risks. They are learning what it is like to be in a group and disagree. They are learning to navigate social dynamics, and modeling by the teacher is crucial in helping them to figure out those dynamics. There is a developmental shift in middle school, during which students begin to challenge their own values and norms. Developing independent thinking and action is critical during this time. Giving students the opportunity to practice independently and in a group setting, but also with the help of a teacher, builds those skills. The exit passes and assessment strategies in the middle school lessons provide students with opportunities to test themselves in a safe environment and also provide teachers with valuable information about whether students have met the objectives and answered the essential questions with accuracy. Each lesson in the toolkit includes the following components:

Rationale: Why use this lesson? This is a statement that identifies the purpose of the lesson and the relevance of the topics discussed.

Objectives: What does this lesson hope to achieve? The objectives address what outcomes can be expected as a result of the lesson.

Standards: How does the lesson align with standards? The standards present themes from the National Council of Social Studies, which have been identified as core concepts in social studies teaching.

Materials: What do I need to use this lesson? This area highlights the handouts and additional resources educators will need to gather, as well as any pre-lesson preparation (e.g., cutting a handout into strips) that needs to occur.

Time: How long will the lesson take? The lessons are developed around a 45-minute class period. The times are for core lesson components, exclusive of extension activities.

Procedures: How do I put the lesson into practice? The procedures include the step-by-step process for completing the lessons. In certain lessons, an alternate strategy may appear which gives a different approach to completing the process. Special considerations or ideas/concepts to address or highlight are indicated in the sidebar of each lesson.

Assessment: How can I informally assess student learning? Ideas for assessment are included, but these are subjective and must reflect the teachers' requirements (see p. 10 for a description of how assessment is approached in the toolkit).

Extension activities: What other ways can I engage students on this topic? Each lesson includes one or more extension activities which provide opportunities to further explore the topic of the lesson.

Standards: How do the lessons align with standards?

Standards are used to ensure a level of consistency in learning concepts across classrooms throughout the United States dealing with the same subject matter. While standards can seem restrictive, the standards outlined by the National Council for the Social Studies (NCSS) are flexible enough to allow teachers and schools room to be creative in how they teach content.

The lessons in the toolkit are aligned with the ten themes outlined by NCSS:

1. Culture
2. Time, Continuity, and Change
3. People, Places, and Environments
4. Individual Development and Identity
5. Individuals, Groups, and Institutions
6. Power, Authority, and Governance
7. Production, Distribution, and Consumption
8. Science, Technology, and Society
9. Global Connections
10. Civic Ideals and Practices

Standards apply specifically to education in the United States but the standards outlined above can be applied to an international education context. For more explanation about each standard, visit http://www.socialstudies.org/standards/strands.

Assessment: How do you assess lessons on peacebuilding and conflict?

The lessons in this guide do not allow for traditional forms of test-like assessment. Conversations that involve personal reflection and understanding multiple perspectives are difficult to assess using quantitative measures. Assessment often takes a more subjective form, for example, through a teacher's observation of a student's participation in activities, small group, and whole class discussions, as well as individual growth. Each lesson offers ideas for assessment, but the decision about how best to assess what students have learned rests with the individual teacher. In the appendices, you will find a sample Participation Rubric which may help in assessing students' level of engagement.

Guidelines for Teaching about Global Peacebuilding

Why teach global peacebuilding?

Teaching global peacebuilding is about educating and engaging global citizens who understand the interconnectedness between their lives and the lives of people around the world, and who are committed to managing conflict at all levels. By teaching global peacebuilding, we can communicate to our students effective strategies for practicing civic engagement and empower them with skills and an understanding that they have a voice and that even one voice can make a difference in the world.

Considerations for teaching about global peacebuilding.

While there is no one way to teach peacebuilding, there are a few things to consider when integrating such complex topics into your curriculum. Many of these considerations will be familiar as good practices in education, but they bear reiterating within the context of conflict management.

Bridge the local and the global. Make connections to students' lives.

Teaching any international issue can be difficult as it may seem very remote to students. They may think, "How does this relate to me?" or "Why should I care?" By making connections to students' own lives, their current lived realities, we can unearth the inherent connections between what happens locally and what happens globally. When we build such bridges and connections for our students, international issues take on a new significance and a greater resonance.

Emphasize multiple perspectives.

Conversations on difficult topics allow us to experience and learn different perspectives. It is, therefore, important for our students to develop the capacity to listen to one another and truly hear what each other has to say.

In the process of conversation, disagreement may occur but this provides students with an opportunity to clarify their own perspectives and consider how other people's views can inform opinions. Disagreement is natural and should be considered a healthy part of conversation. Learning to manage conflict is often about effectively dealing with disagreement before it escalates to violence.

Teach dialogue skills.

Debate is a useful educational exercise and has a place in the classroom when discussing complex topics. However, the process of dialogue can contribute significantly to the classroom climate, encouraging an open mind and developing active listening skills. Unlike debate, which concludes with a winner and involves a process of listening for holes in the opponent's arguments, dialogue assumes there is no winner or loser. In the process of dialogue, listening is for the purpose of enhancing one's understanding of a topic.

Encourage critical thinking.

We should strive to ensure that all students receive an education that is academically rigorous, personalized, relevant, and engaging. Critical thinking is just one of the skills that allows students to:

◆ use inductive and deductive reasoning for various situations;
◆ analyze how parts of a whole interact to produce overall outcomes;
◆ effectively analyze and evaluate evidence, arguments, claims, and beliefs;
◆ analyze and evaluate major alternative points of view;
◆ synthesize and make connections between information and arguments;
◆ interpret information and draw conclusions based on the best information; and
◆ reflect critically on learning experiences and processes.

Today's changing world needs critical thinkers, and students must be given a variety of opportunities to truly engage in lessons, problem solve, and interact with their peers.

Engage students in interactive lessons using creativity.

The methods used to teach international conflict management focus on interaction between learners. Thus, the lessons in this toolkit use a range of methods including role-play, small group work, experiential activities, and large group discussion. The toolkit aims to vary instruction to meet a range of student needs but also to keep students focused and engaged. By using interactive strategies, we seek to move from the abstract to the concrete, encouraging students to make decisions about how they will act when faced with conflict and what can be done to address international conflicts.

Focus on individuals. Translate statistics into people.

Statistics can be very powerful, but when talking about issues that seem incredibly remote to students, we want to get beyond the numbers, humanize the topic, make it personal and, therefore, more real. For example, when a source estimates that there are 300,000 child soldiers in thirty countries around the world (Council on Foreign Relations http://www.cfr.org/human-rights/child-soldiers-around-world/p9331), we can become overwhelmed by the numbers and feel that nothing can be done. But when we learn about the experience of individual child soldiers in Sierra Leone trying to find their families after the war, we can begin to understand their plight and learn about ways to help (UN What's Going on? Child Soldiers in Sierra Leone http://www.un.org/works/goingon/soldiers/goingon_soldiers.html).

Share real stories.

One of the ways we can present statistics with a human face is by sharing real stories. It is important that students hear the voices of people whose lives have been affected by conflict and that they move beyond the abstract to the concrete. It is also important that students hear stories about what USIP does and how it engages with the military and civilians in resolving international conflicts. Stories can create bonds by illustrating shared experiences. A student in a school in the United States might be surprised to hear the hobbies and interests of a young person in a conflict zone—surprised because their interests are so similar. Suddenly, the world becomes smaller. That other person seems less foreign, less remote. Stories can also help clarify concepts that may otherwise seem elusive, making the abstract real. At a deeper level, real stories bring home the impact of international conflict on individual lives by tapping into students' empathy. With stories, the answer to the question, "Why should I care?" becomes more evident. Sharing stories alone will not solve a major international conflict but it is enough to engage people—one tool in the toolbox of understanding international conflict.

Leave students feeling empowered.

Difficult topics like international conflict, which involve human suffering, can be overwhelming for any individual. Often when students learn about a new topic, such as an outbreak of unrest in the Middle East or a refugee crisis in Africa, they receive a wealth of information that leaves them feeling a sense of despair, that the situation is so much bigger than them, and nothing can be done to ameliorate the problem. Educators must think carefully about how to assure students that people around the world care about international issues and are taking action, and pursuing solutions. These concrete and positive examples can alleviate the feeling of despair. But, more important, educators must work with students to leave them feeling empowered, knowing that they, too, can take action as an individual or as a community of young people, and they can make a difference.

About USIP

The United States Institute of Peace (USIP) is an independent, nonpartisan, national institution established and funded by Congress. Its goals are to help:

◆ prevent and resolve violent international conflicts;

◆ promote postconflict stability and development;

◆ increase conflict management capacity, tools, and intellectual capital worldwide.

The Institute accomplishes this by empowering others with knowledge, skills, and resources, as well as by directly engaging in peacebuilding efforts around the globe.

Institute Activities

The Institute approaches its work through four main ways—Think, Act, Teach, Train.

Think: We generate research and applied analysis of international conflicts and we identify best practices and develop international conflict management strategies.

Act: We use decades of experience working in conflict zones to prevent conflict, manage it where it occurs, and assist in the transition from war to peace by using tools and approaches on the ground.

Teach: We engage with students and teachers to think critically about international issues and to develop conflict management skills. We introduce a broad public audience to the challenges and importance of peacebuilding.

Train: We train practitioners in the U.S. and individuals in conflict zones, ranging from civil society leaders to U.N. peacekeepers, on how to use tools and approaches to prevent and manage international conflict.

About USIP's Global Peacebuilding Center

The Global Peacebuilding Center encompasses an exhibit space and education center at the headquarters of the United States Institute of Peace in Washington, D.C., as well as a virtual destination at a dedicated website. Through the exhibits and educational programs offered onsite, and the resources and activities available online, the Global Peacebuilding Center introduces visitors to core concepts in peacebuilding, enhancing their understanding of international conflicts and nonviolent approaches to manage and resolve them. With a particular focus on students and educators, the Global Peacebuilding Center contributes to the development of the next generation of peacebuilders.

SECTION 1

Conflict is an inherent part of the human condition.

Conflict is often perceived as something negative, but conflict is a natural part of our lives. When it is handled effectively, it can provide important opportunities for learning and growth. Conflict is the basis on which democracies are formed. Pluralistic, democratic societies thrive when individuals, groups, and organizations acknowledge a range of perspectives and can manage differences and disagreements productively. Democratic societies are generally able to manage such conflict nonviolently because of strong institutions, separation of powers, rule of law, civil society, a free press, accountability through regular elections, and multiple opportunities for citizen engagement with the government.

In this section, students will think about what peace and conflict mean to them. They will form their own definitions after exploring multiple perspectives. The conclusions they draw will create the basis for their understanding of sections two and three of this toolkit, in which they consider how to manage conflict and use the many tools in the conflict management toolbox.

Lesson 1.1
Defining Conflict

Rationale

Before students can begin to think about how to prevent or manage conflict, they must be able to identify it. This process begins with establishing a definition for conflict. In this activity, students begin to define conflict and explore various interpretations of conflict in order to further their understanding of the subject.

Objectives

1. To consider definitions and interpretations of conflict as a way of forming one's own understanding.
2. To consider whether conflict is positive or negative.
3. To explore the role of conflict in our lives.

Standards

◆ Culture
◆ Power, Authority, and Governance
◆ Civic Ideals and Practices

Time: Two class periods (Part 1–45 minutes; Part 2–45 minutes)

Materials are listed below but this lesson could be done with black/white board and markers.

Materials for Part 1

❑ Sticky notes like Post-It® notes (a different color for each group) or small pieces of paper
❑ Chart paper and markers
❑ Tape (to tape up chart paper, if needed, and to tape small pieces of paper if sticky notes are not available)

❏   *Paragraph Exit Pass* Worksheet (or write it on the board)

❏   Timer or watch/clock

Materials for Part 2

❏   Sticky notes like Post-It® notes (a different color for each group) or small pieces of paper

❏   Chart paper and markers

❏   Tape (to tape up chart paper, if needed, and to tape up small pieces of paper if sticky notes are not available)

❏   *Quotes on Conflict and Conflict Management* Handout (cut into strips)

❏   CD player and CD (of your choice, developmentally appropriate)

❏   *Paragraph Exit Pass* Worksheet (or write it on the board)

❏   Timer or watch/clock

45 minutes

Part 1

Procedures

I. Essential Questions

1.   How can we define conflict?

2.   Why might there be multiple definitions of conflict?

II. Motivation/Introduction (10 minutes)

1.   Explain to students that you are going to share a list of words that can be associated with conflict. Share that each statement will begin with "When I say conflict, you think of . . ." and then a word. Each time you finish the sentence with a new word, they should clap if students think of that word very often; snap if they think of the word sometimes; and stay silent if they do not think of it much at all. Encourage students to look around the room and listen with each word to be aware of their classmates' responses. Note that there are no right or wrong answers for this activity.

2.   Start each statement round with, "When I say conflict, you think of . . ." and use some or all of the following words to finish each sentence: difference, innocent, hurt, anger, win/lose, decision, normal, disagree, guilty, unfair, struggle, right, clash, violence, fight, people, learning, wrong, war, ideas, agreement, against, separate, change, avoid, intervene, help.

When you have finished your sentences, ask for volunteers to finish the sentence with their own words.

3.   Briefly discuss the exercise using some or all of the following questions.

   ◆   Which words had the "loudest" reaction, meaning that many of you associate conflict with the word? Which words had the "quietest" reaction? (write them on the board)

   ◆   Why do you think these words were either frequently associated or infrequently associated with conflict?

   ◆   Is a fight different than an argument? Why do conflicts become violent?

   ◆   Do you think conflict is always bad or negative? Can it be positive or have a good ending?

Note: People view conflicts in many different ways, though often, we tend to think of conflict as something that should be avoided. Yet, conflict is neither positive nor negative by itself; how we choose to respond to conflict makes it positive or negative. In this lesson, students will challenge their notions of conflict in order to develop the skills and awareness necessary to respond to conflicts in positive and constructive ways.

◆ Can you think of a conflict you experienced that ended up being positive and that helped you learn something about yourself or someone else?

III. Teacher Directed (15 Minutes)

1. Divide students into groups of three. See sidebar for grouping suggestions.

2. Introduce the different levels of conflict: personal, local, national, and international. Personal—something that directly involved or impacted you; Local—something that happened in your community, school, state; National—something that happened in the country; or International—something that happened in the world.

3. Provide students with an example of each type of conflict.

4. Ask students to think about and share stories about conflict in their lives. They can think personally, locally, nationally, or internationally. Tell them that while one person is sharing, the rest of the group should listen without interruption and write down key words that run through everyone's stories. Refer back to the exercise "When I say conflict, you think of . . ." for examples.

5. Circulate as groups are sharing.

6. Call out "Switch" every two minutes to ensure that every student gets to share.

7. Distribute sticky notes to each group, with each group getting a different color. Once the groups are done, tell them to share their lists of key words out loud and write each word on a sticky note, writing only one word per sticky note. Direct them to stick all of their group's sticky notes on a piece of chart paper.

IV. Guided Practice (15 minutes)

1. Once all groups have placed their sticky notes on chart paper, have each group share their words with the whole class and hang their chart paper on the wall/board. They can stick the notes directly on the board if you don't have chart paper.

2. After all groups have shared, tell them that they are going to write a definition of conflict using the sticky note words from any of the groups.

3. Tell them that their group needs to decide on their top ten words (as a start) from any of the sticky notes hanging. Once they have decided on their top ten, have one representative from each team come to the front and have him or her take their group's ten sticky notes. There will likely be multiples of some words. If a group wants a word that has been taken, they can write that word on a new sticky note.

4. Tell each group to write their definition of conflict using only the sticky notes they have selected. They may write transition and conjunction words between sticky notes (i.e., the, and, if, etc), and they may gather more sticky notes as they are working, if they need them.

V. Independent Practice (5 minutes)

1. Give time for groups to write their sticky note definitions on chart paper.

2. Once done, hang all of the definitions in the room.

3. To share, each group can read their definition or have the whole class take a Gallery Walk (a walk around the room) of the definitions.

4. Ask some or all of the following questions:
   ◆ What similarities and differences do you see between the groups' definitions?

Note: The U.S. Institute of Peace focuses on conflicts beyond U.S. borders. These conflicts may be interstate (between countries, e.g., Arab-Israeli conflict) or intrastate (between groups within a country, e.g., the Lords Resistance Army and the government in Uganda).

GROUPING SUGGESTIONS

Option 1. Invite students to create a physical expression of how they feel about conflict. Have them look around the room and identify a person who has made a similar expression. Start clapping slowly and tell them with each clap they should take one step closer to their identified classmate/s. If the groups are not the right number, adjust them accordingly.

Option 2. Place a big sign that says conflict in the middle of the room or wear it yourself to personify conflict. Invite students to position themselves in relation to the conflict according to how they tend to respond to conflict. For example, if they don't like dealing with it, they can go to the far end of the room and turn away from the conflict. If they directly address it, they can stand really close to the conflict. Create groups with students according to where they are standing in the room.

Note: USIP's Peace Terms defines conflict as follows: An inevitable aspect of human interaction, conflict is present when two or more individuals or groups pursue mutually incompatible goals glossary.usip.org.

Extension Activity

Do the same "When You Say Conflict, I Think Of . . ." exercise with different words instead of conflict, such as democracy, global citizen, human rights, etc.

- Are these differences important? Why?

5. Have each student put a dot sticker on the definition of conflict they like most or have students verbally identify which definition they like most.

VI. Homework

Distribute the *Paragraph Exit Pass* Worksheet and tell students that for homework they must answer the following question in a paragraph, "Why might there be multiple definitions of conflict?" The paragraph must contain a topic sentence, four supporting details and a concluding sentence. Have students complete the exit pass for homework unless you complete the lesson early, in which case students can complete it in class.

Assessment:

Participation, group definitions of conflict, *Paragraph Exit Pass* Worksheet

Lesson 1.1 WORKSHEET: PARAGRAPH EXIT PASS, Part 1

Name: _____

Exit Pass Question:

Topic Sentence:			
Supporting Detail 1	Supporting Detail 2	Supporting Detail 3	Supporting Detail 4
Summary/Concluding Sentence:			

Cut here ✀ -

Name: _____

Exit Pass Question:

Topic Sentence:			
Supporting Detail 1	Supporting Detail 2	Supporting Detail 3	Supporting Detail 4
Summary/Concluding Sentence:			

45 minutes

Part 2

Procedures

I. Essential Questions

1. What can we learn about conflict through the words of others?
2. Does the definition of conflict always remain the same?

II. Motivation/Introduction (1 minute)

Explain to students that people view and understand conflict in different ways.

III. Teacher Directed (5 minutes)

1. Distribute quotes from the Handout: *Quotes on Conflict and Conflict Management*—one quote to each student—and give them time to read their quotes. You may choose to supplement the list with quotes from your own research.
2. Explain that the goal of this activity is to hear many different quotes about conflict and to end up with the one that best reflects conflict. In order to do this, they will be given the chance to share their quotes with classmates.
3. Tell students that when you begin playing music, students should walk around the room. When the music stops, students should form a group with two to four people standing near them. Each person in the group should read his or her quote out loud to the small group. If students hear a quote they like better than the one that they have, they can ask that person to trade with them. Make note that students do not have to trade their quote if they do not want to, but encourage students to share and exchange in a respectful manner. Students are encouraged to share their opinions about the quotes within their small group and to listen quietly to others.

   When the music starts again, students should move around again and repeat the same process with different peers.

IV. Guided Practice (15 minutes)

1. Set the timer for five minutes.
2. Play the music, stop, give five minutes for conversations and trading.
3. Repeat one or two more times.

V. Independent Practice (10 minutes)

1. After the final round, gather students in a large circle if you have space. Otherwise, students can return to their seats.
2. Go around the circle and have everyone share in 30 seconds the quote they ended up with, what it means to them, and why they chose that quote.
3. Ask students to tape their quote to the sticky note definition of conflict (on chart paper from the previous lesson) that it best matches.

VI. Discussion (7 minutes)

Lead a discussion with the whole class using some or all of the following questions:

- What did you learn from this activity about how different people view conflict?
- Is one view and understanding of conflict more correct than another?
- Why do you think so many quotes exist about conflict?
- Why might different societies have different views about conflict?

VI. Closure (7 minutes)

1. Handout Paragraph Exit Pass.
2. Have students complete a Paragraph Exit Pass by answering the following question in a paragraph, "In what ways has your definition of conflict changed?" Collect the paragraphs as students leave the room or have students complete the exit pass for homework if you do not have time.

Assessment:

Participation, *Paragraph Exit Pass* Worksheet

Note: Conflict by itself is neither good nor bad. Each of us as individuals decides what conflict means to us, and we influence what happens in a conflict based on how we respond to it. Our goal is to learn to respond to conflict in a way that does not involve violence and that can change the situation for the better.

Extension Activities

1. Connect with the art teacher to have students illustrate their quotes.

2. Have students research the person who said the quote and identify the context in which the statement was made.

3. Have students find additional quotes on conflict and share them with the class.

Lesson 1.1 HANDOUT: QUOTES ON CONFLICT AND CONFLICT MANAGEMENT
(cut into strips)

Peace is not the absence of conflict, it is the ability to handle conflict by peaceful means. —Ronald Reagan

Aggressive conduct, if allowed to go unchecked and unchallenged, ultimately leads to war. —John F. Kennedy

Today the real test of power is not capacity to make war, but capacity to prevent it. —Anne O'Hare McCormick

You can't shake hands with a clenched fist. —Indira Gandhi

There should be an honest attempt at the reconciliation of differences before resorting to combat. —Jimmy Carter

If you want to make peace, you don't talk to your friends. You talk to your enemies. —Moshe Dayan

When you negotiate an agreement, you must remember that you are also negotiating a relationship. —Harold Nicolson

A diplomat must use his ears, not his mouth. —Komura Jutaro

Truth springs from argument amongst friends. —David Hume

Don't be afraid of opposition. Remember, a kite rises against; not with; the wind. —Hamilton Mabie

The harder the conflict, the more glorious the triumph. What we obtain too cheap, we esteem too lightly; it is dearness only that gives everything its value. —Thomas Paine

Never ascribe to an opponent motives meaner than your own. —John M. Barrie

An eye for an eye makes us all blind. —Mahatma Gandhi

If war is the violent resolution of conflict, then peace is not the absence of conflict, but rather, the ability to resolve conflict without violence. — C.T. Lawrence Butler, author of *On Conflict and Consensus. A Handbook on Formal Consensus Decision-making* (2000)

Work on developing a cooperative relationship, so when conflict comes, you believe you are allies. —Dean Tjosvold

You can outdistance that which is running after you, but not what is running inside you. —Rwandan Proverb

Difficulties are meant to rouse, not discourage. The human spirit is to grow strong by conflict. —William Ellery Channing

Lesson 1.1 WORKSHEET: PARAGRAPH EXIT PASS, Part 2

Name: _____

Exit Pass Question:

Topic Sentence:			
Supporting Detail 1	Supporting Detail 2	Supporting Detail 3	Supporting Detail 4
Summary/Concluding Sentence:			

Cut here ✂ -

Name: _____

Exit Pass Question:

Topic Sentence:			
Supporting Detail 1	Supporting Detail 2	Supporting Detail 3	Supporting Detail 4
Summary/Concluding Sentence:			

Lesson 1.2
Perspectives on Peace

Rationale

Conflict, when managed effectively, can result in a peaceful solution. However, peace is not static. People must work to build and maintain peace. Like conflict, there are many perspectives and interpretations of what peace is and what it looks like. In this lesson, students will explore varying perspectives on peace and begin to develop their own definition of peace.

Objectives

1. To generate multiple definitions of peace.
2. To explain how one's definition of peace is informed by multiple perspectives.
3. To explain that conflict can be a part of a peaceful society and to understand that peace and conflict can be two sides of the same coin.

Standards

◆ Culture
◆ Individual Development and Identity
◆ Power, Authority, and Governance
◆ Civic Ideals and Practices

Time: Two class periods (Part 1–45 minutes; Part 2–45 minutes)

Materials for Part 1

❏ Markers
❏ Crayons
❏ Colored pencils
❏ *Reflection Exit Pass* Worksheet

❏ Scissors
❏ Poster board
❏ Glue

Materials for Part 2

- ❏ Markers
- ❏ Crayons
- ❏ Colored pencils
- ❏ Newspapers and news magazines
- ❏ Scissors
- ❏ Poster board

- ❏ Glue
- ❏ *Reflection Exit Pass* Worksheet
- ❏ *Paragraph Exit Pass* Worksheet
- ❏ *Drawing Exit Pass* Worksheet
- ❏ *Poem Exit Pass* Worksheet

45 minutes

Part 1

Procedures

I. Essential Questions

1. Is there one way to define peace?
2. How are conflict and peace related?

II. Motivation/Introduction (4 minutes)

1. Ask students to stand if they think there is one definition of peace.
2. Randomly select standing and seated students to explain why they are standing or seated.

III. Teacher Directed (4 minutes)

1. Distribute a blank piece of paper to each student. Have students write their name in the top left corner of the paper.
2. Ask each student to write a definition of peace and then turn the paper over.

IV. Guided Practice (15 minutes)

1. Tell students to draw their idea of peace on the other side of the paper using pictures or symbols. Do not let students use words. Let them know that they will share their drawings with others who will add to them.
2. Stop them after 30 seconds and have them pass the paper to the person next to them.
3. Direct the students to add to what they see on the paper, keeping peace as the theme.
4. Stop them after 30 seconds and have them pass the paper to the person next to them.
5. Direct the students to add to what they see on the paper, keeping peace as the theme.
6. Repeat this process until everyone gets their own drawing back.

   Alternative: If you have a large class, you may wish to divide the class into groups of 8–10 students and have students pass the paper around in their groups.

V. Independent Practice (10 minutes)

1. Ask:
   - What happened to your picture? Does it still reflect your initial definition of peace?

Note: USIP's Peace Terms defines peace as follows: The word "peace" evokes complex, sometimes contradictory, interpretations and reactions. For some, peace means the absence of conflict. For others it means the end of violence or the formal cessation of hostilities; for still others, the return to resolving conflict by political means. Some define peace as the attainment of justice and social stability; for others it is economic well-being and basic freedom. Peacemaking can be a dynamic process of ending conflict through negotiation or mediation. Peace is often unstable, as sources of conflict are seldom completely resolved or eliminated. Since conflict is inherent in the human condition, the striving for peace is particularly strong in times of violent conflict. That said, a willingness to accommodate perpetrators of violence without resolving the sources of conflict—sometimes called "peace at any price"—may lead to greater conflict later glossary.usip.org.

2. Direct students to turn their papers over and revise their definition so that it reflects the revised drawing and now a collective definition of peace.

3. Have each student hold up his/her drawing and read their revised definition from the back.

VI. Discussion (10 minutes)

Lead a discussion using some or all of the following questions:

◆ How did it feel to have others add to your picture and then to rewrite your definition?

• Possible answers might include: feeling unhappy that someone changed their ideas, feeling proud that someone built upon their ideas, feeling anxious about their ideas being changed or about other students seeing their drawing.

◆ What did you notice about the definitions that everyone shared? Were there any similarities or differences? Share that there are many different definitions of peace, just as there are many different definitions of conflict.

◆ What are the consequences when there are many definitions of a concept?

◆ How are peace and conflict related concepts?

◆ Can conflict exist in peaceful societies? What examples of conflict within democratic societies around the world can you think of?

VII. Closure (2 minutes)

Distribute the *Reflection Exit Pass* Worksheet and have students complete it for homework unless you have time remaining in class.

Assessment:

Definitions and drawings of peace, participation, *Reflection Exit Pass* Worksheet

Extension Activity

Peace Symbols: Brainstorm symbols that signify peace (you should have some available to view, including USIP's logo). Have students form pairs to discuss what the symbols mean and have them share the highlights of their discussion aloud. Ask students where they see these symbols. Have students design their own peace symbol using a combination of the more traditional symbols and/or their own peace drawing.

Lesson 1.2 WORKSHEET: REFLECTION EXIT PASS

Name: _____

Question 1: How did you feel about having your definition of peace altered?
Question 2: What are the consequences when there are many definitions of a concept?

Cut here ✂ -

Lesson 1.2 WORKSHEET: REFLECTION EXIT PASS

Name: _____

Question 1: How did you feel about having your definition of peace altered?
Question 2: What are the consequences when there are many definitions of a concept?

Part 2

 45 minutes

Procedures

I. Essential Questions

1. What are the characteristics of a peaceful society?
2. What do you notice about the peace and conflict examples you see in the media?
3. How are peace and conflict related?

II. Motivation/Introduction (5 minutes)

1. Write the following on the board and have students turn to a partner and discuss or have them discuss as a whole class:
   - How would you describe a peaceful society?
2. Randomly select students to explain their answers.

III. Teacher Directed (5 minutes)

1. Explain that students will identify examples of peace in stories from newspapers and then cut those pictures and stories out to make collages on poster board. Students will also have to choose a caption for their collage and explain why they chose their caption. Alternatively, students may use one of their definitions of peace (from the previous activity) as their caption.
2. Divide the class into groups of three to four students.
3. Distribute one poster board and at least two newspapers or news magazines per group.
4. Distribute scissors and glue (enough for each group to complete the activity).

IV. Guided/Independent Practice (20 minutes)

1. Tell students to look through the materials and find examples of peace.
2. Share that when students find an example, they should cut it out of the newspaper.
3. After students have cut out enough examples to form a collage, students can glue their cut outs onto the poster board.
4. Tell students that as a group they must decide what the caption for the collage should be and then explain to the other groups why they chose that caption.
5. Tell students that each group will have one minute to present their caption and collage to the rest of the class.

V. More Guided Practice (15 minutes)

1. Have a representative from each group share their collage with the class and explain their caption.
2. Ask students what they noticed about the collages and captions:
   - What similarities and differences did you notice in the interpretations of peace?
3. To highlight that there can be many interpretations of peace, tell students that they will engage in a quick visual exercise.

Extension Activity

Choose one of the following to complete:

1) Based on what you have learned about peace and conflict, answer this question in a paragraph: What is the relationship between peace and conflict? The paragraph must contain a topic sentence, four supporting details and a concluding sentence.

2) Based on what you have learned about peace and conflict, draw a diagram or picture that illustrates the relationship between peace and conflict. The diagram must have a caption that explains the relationship between peace and conflict.

3) Based on what you have learned about peace and conflict, write a poem that captures the relationship between peace and conflict.

4. Tell students that you will ask a question and they should move to the left side of the room for "No" and the right side of the room for "Yes."

5. Ask:
   ◆ Is peace simply the absence of war?

6. Once everyone has chosen a side, have students in each group discuss among themselves why they are standing on their side, and have one representative from each group share with the class.

7. Think about different conflicts around the world, for example, Iraq, Afghanistan, Democratic Republic of the Congo. What might peace mean to the different groups involved in each of these conflicts? Do you think peace looks the same to each of these groups? Why or why not?

Assessment:

Collage, caption, participation, *Exit Pass* Extension Activity

Lesson 1.2 WORKSHEET: PARAGRAPH EXIT PASS

Directions: Based on what you have learned about peace and conflict, answer this question in a paragraph:

What is the relationship between peace and conflict?

Name: _____

Topic Sentence:			
Supporting Detail 1	Supporting Detail 2	Supporting Detail 3	Supporting Detail 4
Summary/Concluding Sentence:			

Cut here ✂ —

WORKSHEET: PARAGRAPH EXIT PASS

Directions: Based on what you have learned about peace and conflict, answer this question in a paragraph:

What is the relationship between peace and conflict?

Name: _____

Topic Sentence:			
Supporting Detail 1	Supporting Detail 2	Supporting Detail 3	Supporting Detail 4
Summary/Concluding Sentence:			

Lesson 1.2 EXTENSION WORKSHEET: DRAWING EXIT PASS

Directions: Based on what you have learned about peace and conflict, draw a diagram or picture that illustrates the relationship between peace and conflict. The diagram must have a caption that explains the relationship between peace and conflict.

Name: _____

Caption: _____

Lesson 1.2 EXTENSION WORKSHEET: POEM EXIT PASS

Directions: Based on what you have learned about peace and conflict, write a poem that captures the relationship between peace and conflict.

Name: _____

Title of Poem: _____

SECTION 2

Violent conflict can be prevented.

Conflict can be either positive or negative. When it is not managed effectively, conflict can escalate to violence. But violence is not inevitable. In this section, we present some core concepts and skills relevant to the prevention of violent conflict. The goal of conflict management is to find nonviolent solutions to a problem, solutions to which all parties agree. Effective conflict management also strives to build the capacity (via institutions, processes, laws and rules, as well as skills and tools) of societies, organizations, and individuals to resolve disputes and address the sources of conflict in ways that are nonviolent and perceived to be equitable. The process of conflict management, whether at the personal or international level, is dependent upon trust, relationship building, and working cooperatively to find solutions.

Conflict analysis is the starting point for addressing conflict. It is a process through which you can begin to understand a conflict in all of its complexity by identifying the various elements, including parties, issues, relationships, perceptions, definition of the problem, history, roots of the conflict, and structural impediments to a solution. Once you have analyzed a conflict and are aware of the various perspectives involved, the process of imagining creative solutions becomes easier. And once you understand the conflict you can think about how you will approach it. Knowing your conflict style, or how you tend to deal with conflict, and being able to identify the style of the parties with whom you are in conflict can lead you to adjust your behavior in ways that contribute to an effective solution. Another tool for successful conflict management is effective communication, which includes active listening. When one side does not feel as though they are being heard, they may be reluctant to communicate with other parties. By using active listening skills, parties in conflict can build trust in demonstrating that they want to understand the other party. These are core concepts in our field.

Conflict analysis, conflict styles, and active listening are all skills used in the processes of negotiation, in which two or more parties are directly engaged in resolving their conflict, and mediation, in which an impartial third party attempts to assist parties in conflict in finding agreeable solutions. Conflict management, whether interpersonal or international, includes a process of communication. An outcome is never guaranteed. But through the process, relationships can be established that may serve the future needs of all parties involved.

Lesson 2.1
Observing Conflict

Rationale

Conflict analysis is a key process in managing conflict. Through analysis you can begin to understand a conflict's complexity. Once you have analyzed a conflict and are aware of the various perspectives involved, the process of envisioning creative solutions becomes easier. This activity engages students in simple conflict analysis by teaching students what to notice when they observe a conflict. Students learn a more in depth process of conflict analysis in lesson 2.3.

Objectives

1. To understand the value of analyzing conflicts.
2. To identify elements to look for when observing conflicts.

Standards

♦ Individual Development and Identity

♦ Individuals, Groups, and Institutions

♦ Power, Authority, and Governance

Time: One class period (45 minutes)

Materials

❑ *Conflict Role-plays* Handout (only for the pairs role-playing)

❑ *Observing Conflict* Worksheet

❑ *Paragraph Exit Pass* Worksheet (optional)

45 minutes

Procedures

I. Essential Question

What can you observe about conflicts that will help you understand them better and help prepare you to manage them?

II. Motivation/Introduction (5 minutes)

1. If definitions of conflict are still hanging in the classroom from Lesson 1.1 (Part 1), ask students to get up and move to their preferred definition. Have one person at each definition read it out loud. If the definitions are not hanging, ask students what they remember about the definitions of conflict that they wrote. Share with students that they will begin analyzing conflicts as a way to understand them better.

2. Select four students ahead of time to act out Role-play 1 and Role-play 2. Give them time to read the scenarios for understanding. Encourage them to role-play how a conflict can escalate by name calling, yelling, arguing, etc., but remind them that there should be no physical contact or use of force. Tell them they will have 3 minutes to act out their role-play.

3. While the four students are preparing, ask the class if anyone has a brief example of a time they observed a conflict. What did they notice?

III. Teacher Directed (5 minutes)

1. Divide the class into seven groups.

2. Distribute the *Observing Conflicts* Worksheet to everyone and review the questions. Assign each group one question to answer from the worksheet.

3. Tell the class they are going to observe a role-play closely and answer their one question.

IV. Guided Practice (15 minutes)

1. Have the first pair of students present Role-Play 1.

2. After the role-play, direct students to answer their one question independently by writing the answer on a piece of paper. Have them share answers with the people in their group. Have each group select a representative to share with the whole class.

3. In the order of the questions on the worksheet, ask each representative to share their answer.

V. Independent Practice (15 minutes)

1. Explain that students will now have the opportunity to practice observing various elements of conflict on their own.

2. Distribute another copy of the *Observing Conflicts* Worksheet to each student.

3. Share that they are to watch Role-Play 2 and take notes on the worksheet.

4. Have the second pair of students present Role-Play 2.

5. After students have had time to take notes, pair them up to review their notes together and complete the worksheet.

6. Once students have finished, call on pairs to share their answers and discuss any differences of opinion.

Alternate Ending: You can use a version of "Playback Theater" to address the last question of the worksheet: "How could the conflict have ended differently?" Have pairs volunteer to jump into the role of the characters in the second role-play and play back the role-play with their alternate ending. Then explain that this strategy is a model of peacebuilding that has been used throughout the world. Playback theater is a form of improvisational theater that values personal stories and community building. It is used internationally in situations of trauma or crisis, as a means of facilitating community dialogue and as a reconciliation process. Playback theater has been used with refugee populations and with groups, such as the Dalit, or untouchables, in India to address discrimination.

Extension Activity

Using students' homework (*Observing Conflicts* Worksheet based on a personal conflict), have them turn their conflict into a conversation, writing in script format, or a comic strip, but leaving out the ending. Have students exchange their scripts/comics and have a partner write an ending or guess the actual ending.

VI. Discussion or Optional Exit Pass (5 minutes)

Lead a discussion using some or all of the following questions:

- Why is understanding or knowing a conflict well important when trying to find a solution?
- The worksheet is useful for understanding interpersonal conflicts—conflicts between two or more people. How do you think observing conflicts can help you understand a national or international conflict you have studied? What other questions would you ask to help understand a larger or more complicated conflict? Share with students that in lesson 2.3 they will look at a more in depth process that will help them understand more complicated conflicts.

VII. Homework *(optional, as preparation for Lesson 2.2)*

Think about a conflict you have had with another person and analyze it using the *Observing Conflicts* Worksheet. Think specifically about how you handled it and what you could have done differently.

Assessment:

Participation, *Observing Conflicts* Worksheet

Lesson 2.1 HANDOUT: CONFLICT ROLE-PLAYS

Role-play 1

Student A (playing a young person): Your mother/father is not happy with your grades. She/he thinks you are spending too much time with your friends and does not like them. She/he wants to take you out of your current school and put you in a private school so you will focus more on studying. You are very happy in your current school and do not want to leave your friends to go somewhere new. For you, the issue is not your friends, it's the amount of homework you have and the difficulty of the subjects.

Student B (playing a mother/father): Your son/daughter is not doing well at school. You think he/she is wasting too much time with friends who are also not doing well. You want your child to go to the private school in town where there is a stronger academic environment and fewer distractions from studying.

Cut here ✂ -

Role-play 2

Student A (playing a young person): You are sure your sister/brother has borrowed your favorite T-shirt again. You can't find it anywhere in the house.

Student B (playing a young person): You borrowed your sister's/brother's T-shirt. She/he wasn't home, so you couldn't ask her. When you get home from school, your sister/brother is there and very angry.

Lesson 2.1 WORKSHEET: OBSERVING CONFLICT

Directions: Use this worksheet to help you analyze a conflict when you observe it.

1. Describe what happened (the facts).

2. Who was involved?

3. What was the conflict about?

4. What was the problem for person A?

    A feels . . .

    A needs . . .

5. What was the problem for person B?

    B feels. . .

    B needs. . .

6. How did the conflict end?

7. How could the conflict have ended differently?

Lesson 2.1 WORKSHEET: PARAGRAPH EXIT PASS

Exit Pass Question: What is the value of analyzing a conflict and how can you use this skill in your life?

Topic Sentence:			
Supporting Detail 1	Supporting Detail 2	Supporting Detail 3	Supporting Detail 4
Summary/Concluding Sentence:			

Cut here ✄ -

Exit Pass Question: What is the value of analyzing a conflict and how can you use this skill in your life?

Topic Sentence:			
Supporting Detail 1	Supporting Detail 2	Supporting Detail 3	Supporting Detail 4
Summary/Concluding Sentence:			

Lesson 2.2
Identifying Conflict Styles

Rationale

Knowing how you tend to deal with conflict can be helpful in figuring out what you might do differently to manage conflict better or to find a more positive outcome. This activity gives students the opportunity to reflect on how they tend to respond to conflict and to explore the value of using different conflict styles in different situations.

Objectives

1. To understand the value of knowing one's tendencies for dealing with conflict.
2. To understand the value of identifying conflict styles of those with whom you are in conflict.

Standards

◆   Individual Development and Identity
◆   Individuals, Groups, and Institutions
◆   Power, Authority, and Governance
◆   Production, Distribution, and Consumption

Time: One class period (45 minutes)

Materials

❑   *What Do You Do When. . . ?* Worksheet
❑   *Conflict Styles* Handout

45 minutes

Procedures

I. Essential Question

Why is it useful to know what conflict style you use most often?

II. Motivation/Introduction (1 minute)

Explain to students that people respond to conflicts in very different ways and there is no single correct way to respond. Tell students they are going to do an activity that will help them determine how they tend to respond to conflict.

III. Teacher Directed (12 minutes)

1. Distribute the *What Do You Do When. . . ?* Worksheet and have students complete it.
2. Divide the class into five groups and assign each group a number from one to five, which they will use later.
3. In their groups, have students share what patterns they see on their individual worksheets. Do they have a lot of A's, a lot of C's, or a few of each letter?
4. Write the five styles by name on the board (Avoidance, Confrontation, Accommodation, Compromise, Problem Solving). Ask students to guess which style matches each letter on the *What Do You Do When. . . ?* Worksheet (A. Confronting, B. Avoiding, C. Accommodating, D. Compromising, E. Problem Solving).
5. Have them identify their dominant style by looking at their pattern.
6. Distribute the *Conflict Styles* Handout and go over the highlights of each style.

   Alternative Strategy: You may choose to introduce the styles by role-playing a scenario with a student five ways, using a different style each time and asking the class to describe what they saw.

IV. Guided Practice (22 minutes)

1. Tell students that now they are going to see what the styles look like by acting them out.
2. Have each student share in their group a conflict they have been involved with, how they handled it, and how they could have handled the conflict differently using another style. Then have the group select one of the conflicts that they shared to act out. (If you are concerned about the nature of the personal conflicts, you can assign each group one of the scenarios from the *What Do You Do When. . . ?* Worksheet.)
3. Randomly assign each group a conflict style and have them act out the conflict using that style.
4. Give groups time (5–7 minutes) to practice acting out their assigned scenario.
5. Have each group present their scenario/conflict. While each group presents, have the audience identify on the *Conflict Styles* Handout which group (1, 2, 3 . . .) is acting out each style and how they know. At the end of each scenario, have the class share their responses.

VI. Discussion (10 minutes)

Lead a discussion using some of the following questions:

- Why might you use different styles with different people in different situations? Ask for examples.
- Is it possible to use more than one style in a situation, for example, to move from confrontation to compromise? What might make someone move in this way? (If you saw more than one style in one of the scenarios presented, point this out to the group).
- Is one style best for managing conflicts? (Each style has its place, but generally when managing conflict, the problem-solving approach leads to a solution that is agreeable to everyone).
- Why is it useful to know what conflict style you use most often?
- How can it be helpful to know someone else's style?
- What national and international examples (current or historical) can you think of in which you have seen people or groups in conflict use these styles? (Try to relate the styles to the social studies events you have studied with your students).

Extension Activity

Have students draw a symbol/cartoon caricature that represents their conflict style. Post them in the room and have students guess the styles based only on the visual representation.

Assessment:

What Do You Do When? Worksheet, scenarios in groups, *Conflict Styles* Handout, discussion questions, participation

Source for Conflict Styles Grid: K. Thomas, "Conflict and Negotiation Process in Organizations," in *Handbook of Industrial and Organizational Psychology*, ed. M. D. Dunnette and L. M. Hough (Palo Alto, CA: Consulting Psychologists Press, 1992), 660.

Lesson 2.2 WORKSHEET: WHAT DO YOU DO WHEN. . . ?

Read the scenarios below and write the letter of the response that most closely matches what you would do in the situation. You may find that none of the responses reflects exactly how you would respond, so pick the one closest to what you would do. You can use each letter as many times as you want.

A. Try to convince someone of your point or stand up for what you believe. Address the problem directly.

B. Walk away from the situation, ignore the situation, or deny that there is a problem.

C. Do what others want even if you disagree or if it's not what you want.

D. Make a quick compromise.

E. Find a solution that makes everyone happy.

_____ 1. Your mother wants you to help her clean the house on Saturday night and you want to go out with your friends.

_____ 2. Your best friend always borrows your things and never gives them back.

_____ 3. Someone is saying bad things about your friend. You're angry because you know what they are saying isn't true.

_____ 4. You think your teacher has been unfair in grading your test. You think your grade should be higher.

_____ 5. Your friend always wants to copy your homework and it bothers you because it takes you a very long time to do your assignments.

_____ 6. Your friends want to skip school and you don't know what to do. You want to go to school but you don't want your friends to make fun of you.

Lesson 2.2 HANDOUT: CONFLICT STYLES

Directions: Watch each group act out the scenario with a different conflict style. Match the group to the conflict style in the first column. Then fill out how you know in the last column.

Group (1, 2, 3, 4, 5)	Conflict Style	Behavior	Uses	Limitations	How Do You Know?
	Avoiding ◆ Denying a problem ◆ Pretending nothing is wrong	◆ Leaving a situation ◆ Holding back feelings and opinions	◆ When confronting seems dangerous ◆ When you need more time to prepare	◆ The problem may never be resolved. ◆ Emotions may explode later.	
	Confronting ◆ Getting what you want no matter what ◆ Some people win, some lose	◆ Interrupting/ taking over ◆ Ignoring others' feelings and ideas ◆ Loud tone of voice ◆ Sometimes physical violence	◆ When immediate action is needed ◆ When you believe in the absolute rightness of your action and don't see any other choice	◆ This style can make people defensive and can make a conflict worse. ◆ This style can make it hard for others to express how they feel.	
	Accommodating ◆ Giving in to another person's point of view ◆ Paying attention to others' concerns and not your own	◆ Apologizing/ saying yes to end the conflict ◆ Letting others interrupt or ignore your feelings, ideas	◆ When you think you've made a mistake or that you don't really understand the situation ◆ When smoothing over is important for keeping a relationship	◆ You may work hard to please others but never be happy yourself. ◆ Being nice doesn't always solve the problem.	
	Compromising ◆ Each person wins some and loses some	◆ Interest is in finding a solution ◆ Show desire to talk about the problem	◆ When you need a fast decision on a small issue ◆ When nothing else works	◆ You may fix the immediate conflict but not the bigger problem. ◆ Each person may not end up happy.	
	Problem-Solving ◆ Finding a solution that makes everyone happy ◆ Looking closely at the sources of the conflict	◆ Addressing your feelings, needs, and wants ◆ Listening to others	◆ Can make someone who is stubborn move toward resolving a problem	◆ This requires time and good communication skills.	

Lesson 2.3
Practicing Conflict Analysis

Rationale

This activity gives students the opportunity to practice analyzing conflicts using a more in depth process than in Lesson 2.1. Analyzing conflicts enables us to manage them more knowledgably and accurately. Conflict analysis can be used to understand all types of conflicts—between individuals, communities, and countries.

Objectives

1. To understand the various elements of conflict analysis.
2. To understand the value of conflict analysis in managing conflicts.
3. To develop conflict analysis skills.

Standards

◆   Individuals, Groups, and Institutions
◆   Global Connections

Time: Two class periods (Part 1–45 minutes; Part 2–45 minutes)

Materials

❑   *Cross the Line Roles* Handout
❑   *Elements of Conflict* Handout
❑   *Analyzing a Conflict* Worksheet (You will need two copies per group, one for Part 1 and one for Part 2. If possible, save paper by making double-sided copies of the worksheet.)
❑   Newspaper or news magazine articles (one per group of three). BBC.com and NY Times' Upfront Magazine are good sources. USIP also has brief descriptions of conflicts at www.usip.org.

Preparation

Prior to class, cut the *Cross the Line Roles* into strips, so you have enough strips to give each person in the pairs participating in the activity. The observer in the activity does not get a strip.

45 minutes

Part 1

Procedures

I. Essential Question

Why is it important to understand the process of conflict analysis?

II. Motivation/Introduction (25 minutes)

Tell students they are going to practice solving a problem. Conduct the *Cross the Line* activity (see Activity: *Cross the Line* for directions).

III. Teacher Directed/Guided Practice (20 minutes)

1. Ask students what it means to analyze something and what the purpose of analyzing something might be, for example, to understand, to be able to respond, to gain lessons for the future, etc.
2. Distribute the *Elements of Conflict* Handout to each student and review the six elements.
3. Distribute one *Analyzing a Conflict* Handout to each group of three from the *Cross the Line* activity.
4. In their groups, have students answer questions to identify the elements of the conflict they just acted out in *Cross the Line*.
5. Go over the answers as a whole class, having the observer share his/her group's answers.
6. Ask students what conflict styles each group displayed in their situation (relating back to Lesson 2.2).
7. Share that the process of conflict analysis should be used in all types of conflict situations, from personal to international. The analysis is more complex and takes longer for an international conflict, but it is an essential part of trying to figure out what can be done to manage it.

45 minutes

Part 2

I. Independent Practice (35 minutes)

1. Distribute a newspaper or news magazine article about an international conflict to each group. Be sure to provide a range of articles, so different types of conflict can be explored. Distribute one *Analyzing a Conflict* Handout to each group.
2. Have students read the articles in their groups and complete the *Analyzing a Conflict* Worksheet together. Students should use the *Elements of Conflict* Handout to help them answer the questions.

3. When all groups are finished, have students summarize their article and share responses. If the article they have does not provide information that allows them to answer all of the questions on the worksheet, have them research the remaining answers for homework.

    Alternative: If you have difficulty finding current conflicts for which students have enough background context, you can have them analyze a historical conflict you have studied with them. Analyzing past conflicts is helpful practice, but it serves a different purpose. Analyzing current conflicts helps in figuring out how to approach them. Analyzing past conflicts is useful in determining lessons learned. Students can benefit from both exercises.

II. Discussion (10 minutes)

Lead a discussion using some or all of the following questions:

◆   Which questions are harder to answer? Why?

◆   What is the value of analyzing a conflict?

◆   How can analyzing a conflict help you figure out ways to approach it?

◆   Imagine a complicated international conflict like the conflict in Iraq or Afghanistan. How can analyzing the conflict help those who want to build peace in these areas?

◆   What might happen if you tried to resolve a conflict without knowing enough about it?

Assessment:

Cross the Line participation, *Analyzing Conflict* Worksheet

Extension Activity

Show students photographs depicting conflicts and have students identify the level of conflict, i.e. interpersonal, intergroup, intragroup, etc.

Lesson 2.3 ACTIVITY: CROSS THE LINE

Rationale

This is a problem-solving exercise that has two key messages. Problem solving is easier to manage when 1) people work cooperatively rather than competitively and 2) parties in conflict trust one another. The exercise deals with a life in prison sentence and provides a short timeframe for finding a solution (three minutes to create a sense of urgency and for participants to feel the stress that conflict can create). You can change the scenario to something more relatable to students, but be sure to include a sense of urgency. The purpose of the exercise is for students to discover that by working together they can find a solution that benefits everyone (a win-win solution). Problem solving here is a negotiation strategy.

Procedures

1. Divide the class into groups of three and have them stand in different places in the room.
2. Ask for one person in each group to be an observer.
3. Have the other two in each group face each other with a line on the floor or a piece of tape dividing them.
4. Provide each student in the pairs with the statements on the *Cross the Line* Handout.
5. Gather those assigned Student 1 and make sure they understand what they are supposed to do. [Tell them they can use any strategy except physical violence to accomplish their task. Do not tell them what the other group's scenario is. If they ask, "Can I share my scenario?" simply reiterate that they can use any strategy other than physical violence. The solution becomes achievable when each party shares their scenarios with the other, or full disclosure, but you do not want to lead students to this; rather, you want them to figure this out on their own.]
6. Do the same with those assigned Student 2.
7. Tell them that they will begin on "Action" and have exactly three minutes to solve the problem.
8. After three minutes, say "Stop" and have all students return to their seats.

Discussion

Lead a class discussion using some or all of the following questions:

1. How many of you were "saved" at the end of three minutes?
2. What strategies did you use to try to solve the problem?
3. Why were some groups unable to solve the problem? What could you have done differently?
5. How many of you shared your problem with the other person?
6. Have one person in the Student 1 role and one person in the Student 2 role read their scenario. What do you notice about the scenarios? (They're exactly the same.) How would sharing your scenario and knowing that you had the same situation have changed how you approached the conflict?
7. How important was it to trust the person on the other side of the line? Do you think you would share information with someone you don't trust?
8. How might the exercise have gone differently if you had tried to work together to find a solution agreeable to both of you (a win-win solution)? What does the game teach about cooperation versus competition?
9. Share with students that in the next lesson they will learn more about ways to approach conflict. Let students know that you will return to this activity shortly.

Note: The solution is for both people in the pair to cross the line to the other side and to stay on the other side.

Lesson 2.4A
Responding to Conflict: Nonverbal Communication

Rationale

Research indicates that about 80 percent of our communication is nonverbal. Being able to communicate effectively means understanding verbal and nonverbal interactions. In this activity, participants experience what it is like to interact without words to understand the complexity of communication.

Objectives

1. To develop an awareness of how people communicate without words.
2. To develop nonverbal communication skills.
3. To understand the role of nonverbal communication during conflict.

Standards

◆   Culture

Time: One class period (45 minutes)

Materials

❑   *When No Means Yes* Handout

45 minutes

Procedures

I. Essential Questions:

1. How can we communicate without words?
2. Why is nonverbal communication important when responding to conflict?

II. Motivation/Introduction (2 minutes)

Review the conflict management concepts introduced in the lessons in Section 2 that you have used to date, including conflict analysis (2.1, 2.3), conflict styles (2.2), the value of trust (Cross the Line, 2.3), the value of working cooperatively rather than competitively (Cross the Line, 2.3). Tell students that managing conflict whether at the personal or international level depends on building and maintaining trust, working cooperatively, and building relationships. One of the ways to build relationships is by communicating effectively. Tell students that they are going to focus on developing communication skills.

III. Teacher Directed/Guided Practice (15 minutes)

1. Explain to students that they will study nonverbal communication—ways that people communicate without using words. They will begin by arranging themselves in a line according to the month and day (not year) of their birth. But, they will do this WITHOUT talking, writing, or using any props. In other words, students must find another way to communicate. The exercise must be done with the month followed by the day; it will not work if they arrange themselves by day, then month. The teacher may start the exercise by indicating which end of the classroom is January 1 and which is December 31.

2. Give students a moment to think of a strategy to use, and then tell them to begin. From the moment you say "start," the class should be completely silent.

3. When the group believes it has accomplished the task, check how well they did by having each student in line state their birth month and day starting with the person closest to January 1 (at the start of the line). Students who are in the incorrect place should find their correct place in the line. Once they are in the correct order, have them sit in this order for remainder of class.

4. Debrief this exercise with the following questions:
   - How did you find your place in line?
   - Was it difficult? Why or why not?
   - What strategies did you use? How well do you think they worked? Why or why not?
   - What did you do when you tried to communicate with someone who was using a different system of communication? Share with students the importance of finding a common language, especially when trying to manage conflicts.
   - Have any of you ever had an experience when you tried to communicate with someone, but were misunderstood because of a language barrier? How did you respond?
   - Why is it important to be aware of how you communicate nonverbally? How can it be helpful to pay attention to how others communicate nonverbally when in a conflict situation?

Note: Paying attention to your own nonverbal communication can help ensure that you project openness to the person with whom you are in conflict. Noting the nonverbal communication of others can help you identify when someone feels uncomfortable and may lead you to adjust how you interact with them so they feel more secure.

IV. Teacher Directed (9 minutes)

1. Tell students that they are going to read an example of miscommunication over gestures. The story is about a Peace Corps volunteer in Slovakia who had difficulty with nonverbal communication.
2. Have students locate Slovakia on a map and identify the countries that border it. Ask them what they know about the country/region from history, e.g., WWI and WWII.
3. Divide students into groups of three or four and distribute the *When No Means Yes* Handout to each student.

V. Independent Practice (15 minutes)

1. Have students read the story and answer the questions at the bottom of the handout in their groups.
2. Have groups share their responses.

VI. Discussion (4 minutes)

Lead a discussion using some or all of the following questions:

◆ How can nonverbal communication impact negotiations where parties are from different cultures or countries?
◆ How could a peacebuilder prepare him/herself to use nonverbal communication for a negotiation?

Assessment:
Participation in small group work and large group discussion

Extension Activity

Have students create a Top Ten Ways to Communicate Nonverbally poster or a radio advertisement that promotes and explains the importance of nonverbal communication.

Lesson 2.4a Handout: When *No* Means Yes

It's true that the Peace Corps is the "toughest job you'll ever love," but I had no idea it would be the most confusing. Shortly after arriving at my Peace Corps site in Ruzomberok, Slovakia, I decided to visit another Peace Corps Volunteer in a neighboring town. My Slovak was ok, having had three months of language and cultural training, but I still relied on gestures to get around and hadn't yet learned a lot of slang. I walked into the train station to buy a ticket for the short ride to Liptovsky Hradok. To buy my ticket, I told the ticket seller where I was going and held up one finger, my forefinger, to indicate that I wanted one ticket. I was very confused when he gave me two. I shook my head to suggest there was a mistake and gave one back. I didn't realize that in Slovakia you hold up your thumb to suggest one. Holding up your thumb and forefinger means "two." When I showed my forefinger, he assumed I wanted two tickets. Over the course of the next two years, I would mistakenly end up with two movie tickets, two bus tickets, and two train tickets on countless occasions. Old habits die hard.

After I bought my train ticket, I walked out to the platform. I heard some muffled noises from the loud speaker that I could not understand and hoped the announcement wasn't anything important. A train arrived a few minutes later, and I followed the crowd toward it. Before I got on, I asked a woman, "Liptovsky Hradok?" hoping my intonation would explain what I meant. She nodded and said, "*No.*" I stepped back and let others board, returning to the platform to wait for my train. Another train came from the opposite direction and I approached it. Again, I asked someone, "Liptovksy Hradok?" This time the response was *Nie.* Now I was confused. *Nie* means "no" in Slovak, but why had the first woman said "no"? I went into the train station to look at the train schedule. My train had come and gone. I waited for the next train to Liptovsky Hradok, got on it, and hoped it would take me where I wanted to go. When I finally reached my friend's apartment, I told him what had happened. He said that he had recently learned *no* is the quick way of saying Ano (ah-no), which means yes. I thought back to when the woman said no, meaning yes, to me at the first train. She had smiled and nodded, but I had ignored those gestures because the word sounded so familiar to me. But when I relied on gestures like my forefinger to indicate one ticket, that had resulted in confusion, as well. Some things made sense to me, others did not. I wondered if I would ever be able to feel at home in a place where everything seemed upside down.

Note: Words in italics are in Slovak.

Answer the following questions in your groups.

1. What are the sources of the writer's confusion?
2. What gestures does she assume are universal?
3. What would you do in her situation to try to manage the challenges to nonverbal and verbal communication?
4. How can managing these challenges help prevent conflict?

Biography: Alison Milofsky is a senior program officer at the United States Institute of Peace, where she facilitates workshops on communication and negotiation skills. She continues to feel at home in Slovakia, 15 years after leaving the Peace Corps. She visits Ruzomberok every summer with her Slovak husband, whom she met there, and her two children, who speak Slovak and English. She speaks Slovak with her in-laws, but she still occasionally makes the forefinger-equals-one mistake.

Lesson 2.4B
Responding to Conflict: Active Listening

Rationale

Effective communication consists of both speaking and listening. When trying to manage a conflict, using active listening allows you to increase your understanding of the other parties, build trust, and develop or maintain relationships. This activity gives students the opportunity to identify what active listening is and why it is important in managing conflicts.

Objectives

1. To identify key active listening skills.
2. To develop students' active listening skills.

Standards

◆   Culture

Time: One class period (45 minutes)

Materials

❏   *Core Principles of Active Listening* Handout
❏   *Abegaz and the Lion* Extension Handout

45 minutes

Procedures

I. Essential Question
How does active listening play a role in responding to conflict?

II. Motivation/Introduction (3 minutes)
Ask students for situations that require listening. Examples: getting directions, helping a person, learning about someone, listening to music for entertainment, etc.

III. Teacher Directed (15 minutes)

1. Ask two students to act out Scenario 1 (below). Direct the rest of the class to observe the conversation. Give Student A and Student B their instructions privately. If you are concerned about whether your students can act out listening skills, you can play the role of listener in the scenarios.

   Scenario 1: Student A

   Talk about what you did over the weekend. Share a lot of details.

   Scenario 1: Student B

   When your classmate starts to speak, exhibit poor listening skills, such as look at your watch, interrupt, avoid eye contact, look bored or impatient, tap your foot or fidget.

2. At the end of the conversation, draw a T-Chart (an enlarged capital T, with room for writing on each side of the vertical line) on the board and ask the class to describe what the listener was doing.

3. Record their ideas on the right side of the T-Chart.

4. Ask Student A to describe how he/she felt.

5. Ask two students to act out Scenario 2. Direct the rest of the class to observe the conversation.

   Scenario 2: Student A

   Talk about what you plan on doing next weekend. Share a lot of details.

   Scenario 2: Student B

   When your classmate starts to speak, exhibit good listening skills, such as nod, smile, show concern, maintain eye contact, restate what he/she says, ask questions, and encourage.

6. At the end of the conversation, ask the class to describe what the listener was doing.

7. Record their ideas on the left side of the T-Chart.

8. Ask Student A to describe how he/she felt.

IV. Guided Practice (8 minutes)

1. Ask the class if they can figure out what the headings should be for each side of the T-Chart.

2. If necessary, coach them. (Left Side: Active/Good Listening Skills; Right Side: Poor Listening Skills)

3. Distribute the *Core Principles of Active Listening* Handout and review the content with students.

4. Ask:
   - Is there anything we should add to the left side of the T-Chart?

Quick Activity: Lap Sit (10 minutes)

Use this quick trust building exercise if you have extra time in your lesson one day.

1. Have everyone stand in a circle facing their left, so everyone is looking at the back of the person in front of them.

2. Make sure they are very close to each other. If they need to get closer, they can take a step into the circle. This will tighten the circle.

3. Tell students that when you say "sit," they should slowly sit on the lap of the person behind them. The exercise only works if everyone sits at the same time.

4. Have everyone stand and then lead a discussion using the following questions.

   - How did it feel to do this exercise?

   - Was anyone nervous? Why? How did you overcome your nervousness?

   - What was the role of trust in this exercise? What is the role of trust in peacebuilding?

V. Independent Practice (10 minutes)

1. Tell the students that they are going to practice using active listening skills with a partner. Brainstorm with the class a few topics that have multiple perspectives and are often discussed or debated in society. Write these on the board. Divide the class into pairs, assigning one student, Student A and the other Student B. Have each student select a topic on which to speak for two minutes. Instruct students to use active listening skills when they are not speaking.

2. Have Student A speak on their topic for two minutes while Student B listens using active listening skills.

3. After two minutes, have Student A share with Student B what Student B did well. What active listening skills did Student A notice Student B using? Allow two minutes for feedback.

4. Have students switch roles: Have Student B speak on their topic for two minutes while Student A listens using active listening skills.

5. After two minutes, have Student B share with Student A what Student A did well. What active listening skills did Student B notice Student A using? Allow two minutes for feedback.

VI. Discussion (9 minutes)

Lead a whole class discussion using some or all of the following questions:

- What did it feel like to really be listened to without being interrupted? Does that happen often in your life? Why or why not?

- What made this activity challenging for you?

- How can using active listening skills help you to build trust with the person to whom you are listening?

- Why is active listening an important skill for managing conflicts of all levels, from personal to international? What might happen in an international conflict when parties do not feel heard? Revisit the importance of trust and building relationships when managing a conflict. Also explain that active listening allows you to learn the other person's perspective instead of assuming you know what they think/mean/want.

- Ask for volunteers to share one core principle of active listening they do well and one they need to work on.

Assessment:

Participation in whole class and paired activities

Extension Activity 1

Have students complete the same exercise but this time they should think of a personal conflict they had that was not resolved or where they were not happy with the outcome. In pairs have them take turns listening to each other's experiences using active listening skills. The goal of listening in the exercise is to understand the conflict, the perspective of the person sharing with you, and to build trust by being a good listener. The goal is not to solve the problem.

Extension Activity 2
Abegaz and the Lion, a folk tale from Ethiopia

Introduce the concept of oral tradition and folk tales as ways for communities to share important lessons from generation to generation. Abegaz and the Lion is a folk tale from Ethiopia. You can have students read the folk tale by distributing the handout, or you can have them listen to a podcast of the folk tale on the Peace Corps website at http://www.peacecorps.gov/wws/stories/stories.cfm?psid=66##. This story is just one example that may be useful in educating young people about communication.

After they read/listen to the story, discuss the meaning.

1. Abegaz had a big problem. He had to confront a lion. How did he do this? What was his strategy?

2. Why do you think he asked the lion directly for a hair instead of trying to take it? Why did the lion give it to him?

3. Why did the healer send Abegaz to the lion? Why are active listening and effective communication so important for peacebuilding at the personal and the international level?

Note: The story of Abegaz and the Lion ties in very nicely with the lessons that address the importance of trust building and relationship building between individuals and groups in conflict. It can also be used as an extension to the *Cross the Line* exercise in Lesson 2.3.

Lesson 2.4B HANDOUT: CORE PRINCIPLES OF ACTIVE LISTENING

Below are five core principles of active listening.

- Physical Attention
  - Face the person who is talking.
  - Look them in the eye, if it is culturally appropriate.
  - Notice the speaker's body language; does it match what he/she is saying?
  - Can you match the speaker's body language?
  - Try not to do anything else while you are listening.

- Paraphrasing
  - Show you are listening and understanding what is being said.
  - Check the meaning and your interpretation.
  - Restate basic ideas and facts.
  - Check to make sure your understanding is accurate by saying:
    - "It sounds like what you mean is. . . Is that so?"
    - "So what happened was. . . Is that correct?"

- Reflecting
  - Show that you understand how the person feels.
  - Help the person evaluate his or her feelings after hearing them expressed by someone else.
  - Reflect the speakers feelings by saying:
    - "Are you saying that you're angry/disappointed/glad, because. . . ?"
    - "It sounds like you feel. . ."

- Clarifying questions
  - Help clarify what is said.
  - Get more information.
  - Help the speaker see other points of view.
  - Use a tone of voice that conveys interest.
  - Ask open-ended questions, as opposed to yes/no questions, to elicit more information.
    - "Can you explain what you mean by that?"
    - "Can you tell me more about that?"

- Encouragers
  - Show interest by saying:
    - "Really?"
    - "Is that so?"

Lesson 2.4B EXTENSION HANDOUT: ABEGAZ AND THE LION, A FOLK TALE FROM ETHIOPIA

Long ago there lived a young man named Abegaz. He was very, very lonely. Abegaz woke one morning and realized that he could delay the matter no longer. He wanted a wife. Since there were no young women of marriageable age in his village, Abegaz decided to visit a village across the mountainside. Packing up his donkey, he set off in search of a bride.

As Abegaz approached the mountain, he heard the roar of a mighty lioness. Immediately, he jumped off the donkey and ran as fast as he could. Soon, he found himself on the other side of the mountain, with his scared little donkey trailing him. Out of breath, he sat down on a rock that overlooked a peaceful green pasture where sheep were grazing. There, in the middle of the pasture, was a lovely shepherd girl. Abegaz knew instantly that this was the woman he should wed. After introducing himself to her, he asked to meet her father. Within a week, Abegaz was married to the shepherd girl, whose name was Meseletch.

When Abegaz brought his wife home, he was very pleased. No more threadbare pants, no more dirty dishes to wash. Meseletch was as useful as she was beautiful, and Abegaz grew fatter and more content each day.

One day, however, after some years, Abegaz arrived home and Meseletch started to scream. He tried to calm her, but she wouldn't stop. "Be quiet," he said, as he put his hand over her mouth. But Meseletch persisted throughout the night, screaming "Aaagh!" in a high-pitched voice. When the sun rose the next morning, Meseletch's screams had not quieted. Abegaz knew he had to find a cure quickly, so he hastened to the house of the healer.

"Something is wrong with my wife," he told the healer. "She won't stop screaming. Can you give me some medicine to quiet her?"

"I can help you," said the healer. "But first I need a special ingredient. I don't have any lion's hair left. If you'd like me to make the medicine to cure your wife, you will need to climb the mountain, find the lion, and bring me back a single hair from her tail."

Abegaz did not relish the idea of meeting the lion. But he could not bear to go home to his screaming wife. Thanking the healer, he set off for the mountain that he had climbed some years before.

From the foot of the mountain, Abegaz could hear the lion's roars, but he walked steadily in its direction. At last he spotted the lion and, crouching down low, came within 10 yards of her. For many hours, Abegaz watched in silence as the lion chased monkeys from the trees. As he was about to leave, he took a jar of milk from his satchel and placed it in a clearing for the lion.

The next day, Abegaz climbed the mountain once more. This time Abegaz came within a few feet of the lion. Once again he hid behind a tree, watching as the lion closed her eyes and fell asleep. As he left, he took fruit and cheese from his satchel and placed it at the sleeping lion's feet.

On the third day, Abegaz ran up the mountain, carrying a kilo of raw meat. When the lion roared, he said, "Good morning!" and held out his hands to feed her the meat. From that day, Abegaz and the lion became good friends. He brushed the lion's tan coat, helped her chase monkeys, and lay down beside her for afternoon naps.

"May I please take a hair from your tail?" Abegaz asked one day. "My wife needs it."

The lion graciously agreed and plucked a thick hair from her tail.

"Thank you!" Abegaz called, as he ran down the mountain.

"My pleasure," roared the lion.

With the hair in hand, Abegaz knocked on the door of the healer.

"I have it," he said. "I have the hair from the lion's tail." Abegaz told the healer of his friendship with the lion. Then he asked, "What must I do now?" The healer smiled and shook his head, saying, "Abegaz, Abegaz. You have become friends with a lioness, but you still have not made friends with your wife? Who is a better friend, a lion or a wife? Now go home and treat your wife better than that lion."

Source: http://www.peacecorps.gov/wws/stories/stories.cfm?psid=66##

Lesson 2.4C
Responding to Conflict: Negotiation—Identifying Wants and Needs

Rationale

Negotiation is a regular part of everyday life, though it can be difficult to do well. Negotiation skills are extremely valuable in helping people with both shared and opposing interests to reach an agreement. In this lesson, students will learn basic negotiation methods by exploring the difference between positions (what people want) and interests (what people need). Looking to parties' interests instead of their positions can make it possible to find a solution.

Objectives

1. To define negotiation.
2. To understand the difference between wants and needs and identify them in various conflicts.
3. To explore and apply basic negotiation methods.

Standards

◆ Culture
◆ Production, Distribution, and Consumption

Time: Two class periods (Part 1–45 minutes; Part 2–45 minutes)

Materials

❑ *The Homework Conflict Role-play* Handout (two copies for the role play)
❑ *Wants and Needs* Worksheet (one per person in Part 1 and one per person in Part 2)
❑ *Conflict Scenario Role-plays* Handout
❑ *Creating Options* Handout
❑ Dot stickers (optional)
❑ Chart paper

45 minutes

Part 1

Procedures

I. Essential Question

Why is exploring the needs of all parties important in negotiation?

II. Motivation/Introduction (2 minutes)

Ask students to stand if they have ever had to negotiate something. Explain that negotiation is a part of everyday life and that we use negotiation in many different situations.

III. Teacher Directed (15 minutes)

1. Direct students to individually write a definition of negotiation on a piece of paper.

2. Direct them to move through the room and find a partner. Tell them to share their definitions and write one definition together that represents both of their ideas.

3. Direct the pairs to move through the room to find another pair. Tell the pairs to share their definitions and write one new definition together that represents both pairs' ideas. Have groups of four write their final definition on chart paper and post it.

4. Give each student a sticker. Tell them to read all of the posted definitions to themselves and put the sticker on their absolute favorite. If you don't have stickers, you can have students raise hands to indicate which definition they prefer and tally the vote.

5. Ask:
   ◆ "What did we just do?" Take ideas.

6. Share: "We negotiated a definition of negotiation!"

7. Ask:
   ◆ What skills that we have talked about did you use when sharing/writing your definitions?

8. Share with students that negotiation is a process of communication that people engage in to find an agreeable solution to a conflict. We have already worked on a few of the key elements of negotiation: preparation through conflict analysis, ways to approach relationship/trust building through active listening. Now we are going to look at another key element: identifying wants and needs.

   Explain that often when people are in conflict and want something, they state what they want as a position or a demand, for example, "I want a million dollars," "I want you to leave this land," "I want clean drinking water." Demands or wants usually are not flexible, and can make negotiating difficult. Needs are usually underlying and often are not even clear to the person making the demand. Exploring the underlying needs and how to meet these needs is a key skill in managing conflicts. By getting at the needs or why the person is making the demand (why they want what they want), you can often find common ground between parties in conflict, which can open up possibilities for a creative solution.

   If it helps to clarify, you can write the following definitions on the board:

Note: USIP's Peace Terms defines negotiation as follows: The process of communication and bargaining between parties seeking to arrive at a mutually acceptable outcome on issues of shared concern glossary.usip.org.

Note: Not all conflicts can be negotiated. Some conflicts require negotiation as well as other tools. And sometimes people negotiate simply as a way to maintain positions, with no intention of finding a collaborative solution.

Quick Activity: Creating Options

This is a quick activity to practice the brainstorming process, which is helpful in generating creative solutions.

Procedures

1. Ask students:

   a. What does brainstorming mean? How would you describe the process?

   b. How do you think brainstorming can be used in the process of negotiation?

2. Share with the group the ground rules for brainstorming:

   a. All ideas are encouraged

   b. Record all contributions without discussing their merits

   c. Avoid judging any options

   d. Avoid focusing on differences between ideas

   e. Combine related ideas

   f. Do not attach names to ideas

   g. Encourage creativity

   h. Keep the flow going for as long as possible

3. Divide students into small groups and distribute the *Creating Options* Handout to each group. Have students brainstorm in their groups how they can solve the problem.

(continued on next page)

Wants: In a negotiation, a want is a statement of demand and is often not flexible. The party making the demand insists on getting what they want: "I want land" or "I want $500!"

Needs: In a negotiation, a need is what lies beneath the demand and can often be determined by asking *why* a party is making such a demand: "I need to feed my family" or "I need to feel respected."

IV. Guided Practice (15 minutes)

1. Select two students to act out the homework scenario and give them the *Homework Conflict Role-play* Handout. Prepare them by reviewing the conflict with them, making sure they understand their roles.

2. After they have acted out the role-play, ask the class:
   ◆ Do you think they solved their conflict effectively? Why or why not?
   ◆ Did you know their needs?

3. Allow the class to ask the two students anything they want that will help them determine the wants and needs of the siblings. Remind them that asking why someone wants what they want can often get at their needs.

4. Distribute the *Wants and Needs* Worksheet and have students fill in the first three columns on the chart based on the class discussion.

V. Independent Practice (13 minutes)

1. Divide the class into groups of three.

2. Direct them to solve the problem (the last column on the chart-Action), reminding them that the key to finding the best course of action is to understand each person's needs. Refer back to the posted definitions. Have groups share their solutions.

3. Discuss some or all of the following questions:
   ◆ Why do we often focus only on people's wants?
   ◆ Why is it sometimes hard to know someone's needs?
   ◆ How did looking at needs help you think of a solution?

4. Have each group share their solutions and create a master list on the board. One possible solution is to let some of the air out of the tires so the truck can pass through the tunnel. Do not share this solution until the end.

5. If you have time, you can move past the brainstorming phase to the analysis phase in which people talk about the advantages and disadvantages of each idea, as a way of eliminating those that won't work and narrowing the possibilities.

5. Lead a class discussion using some or all of the following questions.

   ◆ Was it difficult to list options without evaluating or analyzing them as you went along? If so, why?

   ◆ Did you have more ideas as a group than you would have had working individually? Why?

   ◆ What is the value of creativity in the negotiation process?

Note: It is often difficult for students to avoid commenting, either positively or negatively, on various ideas. Try to discourage students from doing so. Remind them that after all ideas have been expressed, they can discuss the merits of each.

Part 2

 45 minutes

I. More Independent Practice (32 minutes)

1. Divide students into pairs and give them one of the three conflict scenarios from the *Conflict Scenario Role-plays* Handout to role play. Also distribute the *Wants and Needs* Worksheet to each student.

2. Have each student read their role and identify their own wants and needs. They should write this information under Party 1 on the chart. (5 minutes)

3. Then have each group role play their scenario, trying to determine the other party's wants and needs. Remind them to ask the other party *why* they want what they want. Have them write this information under Party 2. (7 minutes)

4. Have them work together to see what they could do to solve their problem in a way that meets both of their needs. They should put this information under the Action column. (10 minutes)

5. Have one pair from each conflict scenario present their information to the group. After each presentation, ask other groups with the same scenario to add any additional information to the chart. (10 minutes)

Extension Activity 1

Have students work in pairs to create their own conflict scenario. Have students pass their scenario to another individual or pair with the instructions to identify parties, wants, needs, and actions.

Extension Activity 2

Show USIP's witness video on Betty Bigombe and her work negotiating peace in Uganda (www.buildingpeace.org) or George Mitchell and his work in Northern Ireland (www.buildingpeace.org). Have students complete a wants/needs/action chart about the conflict in the video. Have students research the conflicts in the videos to add information to their charts.

II. Discussion (13 minutes)

Lead a class discussion using some or all of the following questions:

◆ Two of the scenarios were interpersonal and one was international. Based on each group's comments, what similarities and differences did you notice among the wants and needs in the two types of conflicts?

◆ Why is exploring needs important in negotiation?

◆ How can looking at needs improve your relationship with the people with whom you are in conflict?

◆ Have students think of examples of local, national, and international conflicts in which people have stated their wants or demands. How has this affected the conflict? Try to tie wants and needs into the historical conflicts you have studied or are studying.

Assessment:

Participation, *Wants and Needs* Worksheet

Lesson 2.4C HANDOUT: THE HOMEWORK CONFLICT ROLE-PLAY

Directions: Read the scenario. Decide who will play each part. Prepare to act in front of the whole class!

Two siblings have assignments to complete for school and both want to use the computer at home. They start arguing over who should be able to use it. The older sibling has an important essay due the next day. The younger sibling has to email his/her science group and send materials by a certain time so the other group members can do their part of the project.

Lesson 2.4C WORKSHEET: WANTS AND NEEDS

Directions: Fill in the first three columns based on the role play and discussion.

	Parties: Who is the conflict between?	**Wants:** What are the parties demanding?	**Needs:** Why does each party want what they are demanding? What do they need?	**Action:** What could each side do in order to get what they need?
Party 1 (name)				
Party 2 (name)				

Lesson 2.4C HANDOUT: CONFLICT SCENARIO ROLE-PLAYS

Role Play 1: Studying or Practicing

Student A

You are studying for a math test and like to study in complete silence. Your sibling is practicing his/her instrument. You want your sibling to stop practicing so you can study.

- -

Student B

You are practicing your instrument for a concert tomorrow. Your sibling wants you to stop practicing because he/she wants to study for a math test in silence.

Role Play 2: Marrying Outside of One's Culture and Religion

Student A

You want to marry someone who is from another culture and religion. Your parents are very against this and want you to marry someone from your own culture and religion. You feel it is most important that you marry the person you love.

- -

Student B

Your son/daughter wants to marry someone who is very nice but does not share your culture or religion. You want your son/daughter to be happy but it is more important that the family maintains your cultural and religious identity.

Role Play 3: The Pampas in Aguala: A fictional case

The Pampas are an indigenous group in the country of Aguala. They believe that the land belongs to those who work it. They work the land, in other words, they grow food on the land and they eat what they grow. The government of Aguala wants the Pampas to move to a different part of the country because they would like to convert the land the Pampas are living on into a site for ecotourism. The Pampas refuse to leave because, as an indigenous group, they have the right to stay on their land.

Student A

You are a representative of the Pampas, an indigenous group in the country of Aguala and have been asked to meet with a representative of the government of Aguala. You believe that the land belongs to those who work it. You work the land, in other words, you grow food on the land and you eat what you grow. The government wants you to move to a different part of the country because they would like to convert the land you are living on into a site for ecotourism. You refuse to leave because, as an indigenous group, you have the right to stay on your land. Also, you don't trust the government because in the past they have made promises to other indigenous groups that they have failed to keep.

- -

The Pampas are an indigenous group in the country of Aguala. They believe that the land belongs to those who work it. They work the land, in other words, they grow food on the land and they eat what they grow. The government of Aguala wants the Pampas to move to a different part of the country because they would like to convert the land the Pampas are living on into a site for ecotourism. The Pampas refuse to leave because, as an indigenous group, they have the right to stay on their land.

Student B

You are a representative of the government of Aguala and have asked to meet with a representative of the Pampas who are an indigenous group in your country. They believe that the land belongs to those who work it. They work the land, in other words, they grow food on the land and they eat what they grow. You want them to move to a different plot of land because you would like to convert the land the Pampas are living on into a site for ecotourism. The Pampas refuse to leave because, as an indigenous group, they have the right to stay on their land.

Lesson 2.4C QUICK ACTIVITY HANDOUT: CREATING OPTIONS

Scenario:

Two truck drivers are driving on a highway to deliver a shipment of humanitarian aid (food, water, medical supplies) to a village that has been devastated by violent conflict. While driving, the drivers pass beneath a bridge. The top of the bridge is not high enough, so their truck gets stuck and the top of the truck gets badly damaged. Cars slowly begin to back up behind the truck, and the line is almost 2 kilometers long. One of the truck drivers thinks that they should continue going forward and force the truck through the tunnel, even if they will damage the top and some of the aid. The other truck driver thinks that they should reverse, even if the traffic behind will make it very difficult.

◆   What else could they do?

Lesson 2.4D
Responding to Conflict: Negotiation Role-play

Rationale

This lesson allows students to practice all of the skills introduced in the toolkit thus far: conflict analysis, conflict styles, active listening, building relationships/trust, identifying wants and needs, and using creative problem solving in one exercise. The scenario is set in Kosovo to get students to think about how these skills can be used in conflicts that range from personal to international settings. However, the conflict could occur anywhere. If you feel that providing background on Kosovo will prove too difficult or time-consuming, you can change the setting to something more familiar to students.

Objectives

1. To improve students' negotiating skills.
2. To apply key negotiation principles and skills in an international conflict setting.

Standards

◆ Individual Development and Identity
◆ Power, Authority, and Governance
◆ Global Connections

Time: Two class periods if you do all of the preparation in class (one class preparation, one class role-play and discussion); one class period if you have students do their preparation at home and choose not to have them meet in like-role groups.

Materials

- ❏ *Analyzing a Conflict* Worksheet
- ❏ *Negotiation Preparation* Worksheet
- ❏ *Negotiation Note-Taking* Worksheet
- ❏ *Competing for a UNMIK Contract in Kosovo Scenario* Handout
- ❏ *Competing for a UNMIK Contract in Kosovo Roles* Handout
- ❏ Source for background on conflict in Kosovo: http://news.bbc.co.uk/2/hi/special_report/1998/kosovo/305008.stm

45 minutes

Part 1

Procedures

I. Essential Question:

How are negotiation skills useful in daily life?

II. Motivation (5 minutes)

1. Ask students to share with a partner one skill they have that makes them an effective negotiator.
2. Ask for volunteers to share their answers with the class.

III. Teacher Directed (25 minutes)

1. Tell students that they will have the opportunity to practice their negotiating skills with a partner in a role-play.
2. Depending on the level of your students' prior knowledge, review the conflict in Kosovo. You may wish to use the *Conflict Analysis* Worksheet to help them analyze the conflict in Kosovo. The negotiation scenario does not have enough detail to allow for a thorough conflict analysis (students can also do this the night before for homework).
3. Distribute the *Competing for a UNMIK Contract in Kosovo Scenario* Handout and review it with the class. Address any questions. (Again, you can distribute the scenario the day before and have students review it for homework in preparation for this lesson.)
4. Remind students of the key elements of negotiation: be prepared (conflict analysis Lesson 2.3), build a relationship and trust (use active listening skills Lesson 2.4b), think about how you want to approach the conflict (what conflict style will you use Lesson 2.2), identify wants and needs (Lesson 2.4c), look for creative solutions (Lesson 2.4c).
5. Divide students into pairs and assign one person in each pair the role of the body repair shop owner and the other the engine repair shop owner. Give students the appropriate role from the *Competing for a UNMIK Contract in Kosovo Roles* Handout.

   Alternative: Depending on the skill level of your students, you might choose to have the negotiation occur in groups of four, two body shop owners and two engine repair shop owners. This allows students to work together in their roles and during the negotiation they can take breaks to discuss strategy among themselves.

> **Note:** This role-play based on Kosovo is an example of an interpersonal conflict taking place in a larger conflict.

IV. Guided Practice (15 minutes)

Preparation: Have the body repair shop owners meet on one side of the room and the engine repair shop owners meet on the other side. Have them work cooperatively to complete the *Negotiation Preparation* Worksheet.

Part 2

🕐 **45 minutes**

Procedures

I. Independent Practice (20 minutes)

Have everyone return to their negotiation pairs (or quads) and begin their negotiation. Give students 20 minutes to negotiate.

II. Discussion (25 minutes)

Lead a whole class conversation using some or all of the following questions:

♦ What were some of the results of your negotiations?

♦ What strategies/conflict styles did you use?

♦ What were some of the challenges you encountered while negotiating?

♦ How were you able to get beyond wants to needs?

♦ What did you learn from the role-play that will help you in future negotiations?

♦ Ask students what they know about the negotiation processes involved in the conflicts they have studied in class. If they have not studied this aspect of the conflict, have them research it.

Extension Activity

Have students research a current international conflict to see what negotiation efforts have been made. Have them report on the processes and share what challenges they see.

Lesson 2.4D WORKSHEET: ANALYZING A CONFLICT

1. Describe the conflict in one sentence.

2. What type of conflict is it? (internal, interpersonal…)

3. **ISSUES:** What are the sources of the conflict? (e.g., resources, values, needs)

4. **PARTIES:** How many parties (different individuals or groups) are involved in the conflict? List them.

5. **RELATIONSHIP:** Describe the relationship among the different parties.

6. **HISTORY:** What is the history of the conflict? How long has the conflict been going on? Is it recurring? How serious is the conflict?

7. **STYLES:** How are the parties currently dealing with the conflict?

8. **MANAGEMENT:** What can the parties do to move toward ending the conflict?

Lesson 2.4D WORKSHEET: NEGOTIATION PREPARATION—COMPETING FOR A UNMIK CONTRACT IN KOSOVO

Directions: To prepare for your negotiation, answer the questions below.

What is your goal for the negotiation? What do you want to get out of it?

What are the key issues for you?

What do you want? What are your needs?

What strategy or conflict style will you use as you approach the negotiation?

Lesson 2.4D WORKSHEET: NEGOTIATION NOTE-TAKING

Directions: While you are negotiating, try to gain the following information.

What does the other party want?

What does the other party need (why do they want what they want)?

What conflict style are they using (competing, accommodating, avoiding, compromising, problem solving)?

What creative ways to solve the problem can you think of? How can you find common ground between their needs and yours?

Lesson 2.4D HANDOUT: COMPETING FOR A UNMIK CONTRACT IN KOSOVO SCENARIO

Background:

The place is Kosovo. The time is 2002. Terrible road conditions combined with a huge influx of émigrés returning from Eastern Europe after the war have resulted in thousands of abandoned cars scattered all along the highways.

Although the economy is starting to revive, farmers on their way to the market place and others are having trouble picking their way through the twisted hulks. The wrecks are slowing the movement of many actors in the reconstruction efforts. The United Nations Mission in Kosovo (UNMIK) has decided they will issue a contract for clean up. A body repair shop wants and needs this contract as does an engine repair shop. The two shop owners see each other in the UNMIK office when they go to submit their bids for the contract.

Lesson 2.4D HANDOUT: COMPETING FOR A UNMIK CONTRACT IN KOSOVO ROLES

Body repair shop owner: You are the proprietor of a body repair shop. You have five children and a spouse to support. Because of the war, many cars have been damaged. While you can bang out crushed doors and bent fenders on most of the vehicles, some of the damaged frames are beyond repair and you need the parts from the European manufacturer. You are unable to fill many orders because it is so difficult to get the panels and parts. Your family's needs are mounting.

You have learned that the United Nations has issued a request for bids to haul away the wrecked and abandoned cars. This could be your opportunity to find many of the parts you are missing. You have decided to go to the UNMIK office today to put in your bid for the contract. You heard that there is another person from your area who is seeking the contract. You recognize him/her when he enters the waiting room. You wish you could dissuade him/her from bidding on the contract or appeal to him/her because the needs of your family are so great, but you are too proud. You decide you will try to negotiate and drive some kind of bargain with him/her.

- -

Engine repair shop owner: You are the proprietor of an engine overhaul company. Many cars are in need of repair after the war, but it is impossible to find parts. You are only able to fix the engines of a few. You need the new parts from the European manufacturers. You are unable to fill many backorders. You have elderly parents and a family to care for.

You have learned that the United Nations has issued a request for bids to haul away the wrecked and abandoned cars in your vicinity. This could be your opportunity to find many of the parts you are missing. You have decided to go to the UNMIK office today to put in your bid for the contract. You heard that there is another person from your area who is seeking the contract. You recognize him/her when he/she enters the waiting room. You wish you could appeal to him/her or dissuade him/her from bidding on the contract because the needs of your family are so great, but you are too proud. You decide to try to negotiate and drive some kind of bargain with him/her.

Lesson 2.4E
Responding to Conflict: Mediation

Rationale

Mediation has been used as an effective method of alternative dispute resolution in many contexts, ranging from neighbor disputes to conflicts between nations. Mediation training provides students with the skills and processes for them to help others take responsibility for resolving their conflicts, and to find peaceful solutions to conflicts in their own lives. In this lesson, students will learn about the mediator's role as a third party and begin practicing skills to assist parties to negotiate solutions to their conflict.

Objectives

1. To understand the role of a mediator in resolving disputes.
2. To identify the basic skills and processes used by effective mediators.
3. To develop basic mediation skills and implement processes.

Standards

◆ Individual Development and Identity
◆ Power, Authority, and Governance
◆ Global Connections

Time: Two class periods (Part 1–45 minutes; Part 2–45 minutes)

Materials

❑ *Mediation Process* Handout
❑ *Mediator's Instructions* Handout
❑ *Mediation Preparation for Disputants* Worksheet
❑ *Mediating Conflict Roles* Handout

45 minutes

Part 1

Procedures

I. Essential Question

What are the differences between negotiation and mediation and when is it appropriate to use the latter?

II. Motivation (5 minutes)

Ask students to think about a situation in their lives when two people or groups were having a disagreement, and though they were not part of the conflict, they tried to help the parties solve it. What skills did they use in order to help solve the problem? (For example, active listening skills, problem solving, etc.) Invite students to share their answers.

III. Teacher Directed (25 minutes)

1. Ask students if they have heard of mediation as a conflict resolution process and if they can define it. Write their responses on the board. Then, write the following USIP definition of mediation (from Peace Terms):
   Mediation is a mode of negotiation in which a mutually acceptable third party helps the parties to a conflict find a solution that they cannot find by themselves.
   Invite a student to read the definition out loud. Ask students what they think third party and mutually acceptable mean. Explain that third party refers to someone who is not a party to the conflict, or is outside of the conflict.

2. Note that mediators try to be impartial but being impartial doesn't mean you don't have an opinion. Everyone has an opinion. The mediator, however, is not supposed to share his/her opinion on the situation, so that parties come to an agreement on their own. Most mediations are voluntary, meaning everyone, including the mediator, can leave the process at any time. In interpersonal settings, mediation is confidential but in international settings this is not always the case. A mediator may choose to use the media to put pressure on the parties in conflict.

3. Lead students in a dialogue with the following question:
   ◆ Why is it sometimes helpful for someone outside a conflict to help parties find a solution? Responses can include the following: the parties are very emotional about the issue, they are uncomfortable dealing with the issue without someone else present, the parties are no longer communicating, or they can't get past their demands/positions.

4. Explain to students that for many different conflicts, trained mediators are asked to help others resolve their own conflicts in a peaceful and constructive way. For example, many schools as well as community centers offer mediation services to resolve conflicts between families, neighbors, students, or community members. Mediators can be of any age, including students, as long as they've been trained in basic mediation skills and processes. On an international stage, warring countries may turn to notable peacebuilders, such as diplomats or retired heads of state, to mediate an international conflict, or conflict between political groups within a country.

♦ What other people, organizations, or countries can you think of that have served as mediators in conflict?

5. Explain that regardless of whether the conflict is between individuals, groups, or countries, peacebuilders can follow a basic process to mediate conflict between parties. Distribute the *Mediation Process* Handout and review each step.

IV. Guided Practice (15 minutes)

1. Share that students will now have a chance to practice a basic mediation. Inform them that this will be an opportunity for them to practice skills from their previous lessons: active listening, identifying wants and needs, and problem solving. Remind them that as a mediator, they must be conscious of verbal and nonverbal communication to maintain the role of an impartial third party.

2. Divide the class into groups of three or four. Instruct each group to identify a mediator (or two co-mediators if it is a group of four), and two parties to the conflict. If moveable seating is available, instruct them to set up three chairs in front of the room in the shape of a triangle—the two parties in conflict sitting side by side facing the mediator. Distribute roles to each group from the *Mediating Conflict Roles* Handout. There is no separate scenario background for students to read, as each role establishes the conflict.

3. Have students meet in like role groups (all mediators together, all Parties 1 together, and all Parties 2 together) and spend ten minutes preparing for the mediation. Distribute the *Mediator's Instructions* Worksheet to the mediators. They should use this during the mediation. They can use the the *Mediation Process* Handout as well. Distribute the *Mediation Preparation* Worksheet to Parties 1 and 2 to complete in their role groups.

Part 2

I. Independent Practice (25 minutes)

Have students return to their mediation triads/quads and give them twenty-five minutes for the mediation.

II. Discussion (20 minutes)

After the role-plays, lead a group discussion:

♦ What was the final result of your mediation? Did you have a chance to come up with any solutions? If not, what do you think possible solutions could have been?

♦ What was either easy or challenging about being a mediator?

♦ For the parties in conflict, what was it like having someone mediate your dispute?

♦ What skills do you think you already have that are useful as a mediator? What skills do you feel you need to work on?

♦ How can developing mediation skills help you in being everyday peacebuilders?

♦ How might the mediation be more challenging if the conflict were international and involved warring parties? What obstacles might the mediator have to overcome?

 45 minutes

Lesson 2.4E HANDOUT: THE MEDIATION PROCESS

Below is the basic five-step process for a formal mediation process, though elements of these steps could be used to informally mediate disputes.

Orientation

The mediator explains the mediation process and establishes trust and mutual understanding with the parties.

◆ Explain the 5 steps of the mediation process to the parties.

◆ Establish ground rules *(for example, no yelling, cursing, or physical contact, one person talks at a time).*

◆ Begin the dialogue session.

"I'm going to take a moment to explain the mediation process and my role in it to make sure everyone understands the process."

1. *I am impartial in this process. My job is to listen, ask questions, and clarify what is important. In this case, I won't give advice, decide who's right or wrong, or take sides. As a mediator in this process, I maintain confidentiality, except in cases of abuse or threats of violence. This mediation is voluntary. We are all here of our free will and can end the process at any time.*

2. *I will explain the process (what I'm doing now).*

3. *You will both tell me about the conflict and I will ask questions for clarification.*

4. *We will define success by developing some criteria against which we can evaluate possible solutions.*

5. *You will all look for creative solutions.*

6. *You will evaluate the various solutions to see which meet the criteria we have defined.*

7. *When you find areas of agreement, we can write them down and everyone can sign it if you like and get a copy.*

1. Exploring Interests (storytelling):

The mediator invites each party to take turns talking about the conflict in their own words (telling their story), asks questions for clarification, and paraphrases the feelings and issues the parties express to ensure understanding. The purpose here is to identify needs so parties feel heard.

"At this point, I will ask you both to speak about issues that brought you to mediation. Then I will check to make sure I understand what everyone has said. I will then ask questions to get a better understanding of what you want to discuss in mediation. Who would like to begin?"

2. Defining Success (moving from negative statements to positive statements of needs)

The mediator should recognize the wants, acknowlede the emotions/grievances, and then reframe the needs. He/she reframes the parties' statements, going from accusations or concerns to statements of needs. These needs can be used as criteria to evaluate different options. In this process, the role of the mediator is to find criteria that will lead to a compromise.

Example 1

Party: Would you want to play next to this garbage dump?

Mediator: It sounds like you are worried about your safety.

Criteria: Any solution to this problem must provide for your safety.

Example 2

Party 1 to Party 2: This is a waste of my time. You decided what you were going to do before you even got here.

Mediator: It sounds like you want to make sure that when we ask for your input and you give it, you can actually influence the outcome.

Criteria: The process to negotiate a solution must include all voices. The agreement must reflect input from all parties.

3. Developing Options (brainstorming)

Once issues have been identified and criteria for success have been established (in Example 1, any solution to this problem must provide for your safety), the mediator can help the parties brainstorm as many options as possible, encouraging creativity.

"Now we are moving into the problem solving phase. While earlier you may have been focusing on the past, during the rest of the mediation we will focus on finding solutions for the future. Starting with the _____ issue, what are some things you could do to resolve this conflict? Be creative, and think about things that you personally can do. I will write them all down. Please don't critique or eliminate others' ideas as you hear them. You will have a chance to evaluate them to search for agreement later."

◆ Brainstorm and list possible solutions. Write them as an action possibility, using verbs and names. For example: Personal conflict: Samuel will start a part time job. Intrastate conflict: The North and South will share power in the government.

◆ Encourage parties to reflect on solutions that will improve and define their future relationship. *"You've both mentioned needing _____. What can you do together to achieve that?"*
Once all the possible solutions are written down, one topic at a time, ask parties to identify which of the solutions they can both agree to and circle it on the list.

4. Evaluating and Selecting Options

The mediator then seeks areas of common interest and helps parties negotiate which solutions they would be willing to accept. For example, for the topic of curfew: *Josh will return home by 10 pm on weekdays. Mom will lend Josh the car on weekends to drive home in the evenings.*

5. Agreement Testing and Writing

Once parties have identified areas of agreement, in this next phase, before writing a formal agreement for them to sign, the mediator makes sure the agreement areas are specific and realistic, and satisfy some of the needs of all parties. It is important to remember, however, that most sustainable agreements will require compromise on all sides.

"At this point, we'll take the items you've agreed to and put them in writing for you to sign if you want."

Lesson 2.4E HANDOUT: MEDIATOR'S INSTRUCTIONS

Mediator:

Conflict: You will be mediating a conflict between two bunkmates at summer camp. Party A, Rachel/Richard, and Party B, Natalie/Nathan are bunkmates who are not getting along. Both want to find a new cabin or a new bunkmate but this is not possible, as there is no other space available in the camp.

Directions: Start off the mediation with the following introduction. Then, listen to each party's perspective using active listening skills to identify their feelings, values, and topics to be resolved in the mediation, and make sure each party feels heard and understood.

"I'm going to take a moment to explain the mediation process and my role in it to make sure everyone understands the process."

1. *I am impartial in this process. My job is to listen, ask questions, and clarify what is important. In this case, I won't give advice, decide who's right or wrong, or take sides. As a mediator in this process, I maintain confidentiality, except in cases of abuse or threats of violence. This mediation is voluntary. We are all here of our free will and can end the process at any time.*
2. *I will explain the process (what I'm doing now).*
3. *You will both tell me about the conflict and I will ask questions for clarification.*
4. *We will define success by developing some criteria against which we can evaluate possible solutions.*
5. *You will all look for creative solutions.*
6. *You will evaluate the various solutions to see which meet the criteria we have defined.*
7. *When you find areas of agreement, we can write them down and everyone can sign it if you like and get a copy.*

"At this point, I will ask you both to speak about issues that brought you to mediation. Then I will check to make sure I understand what everyone has said. I will then ask questions to get a better understanding of what you want to discuss in mediation. Who would like to begin?"

Ensure each party shares their perspective without interruption. Then, using the reflective listening chart, seek understanding of their views by paraphrasing what they each said, and asking questions to clarify their feelings and determine the needs which will help you identify the issues to be resolved.

Lesson 2.4E WORKSHEET: MEDIATION PREPARATION FOR DISPUTANTS

Directions: To prepare for your mediation, answer the questions below.

What is your objective in the mediation? What do you hope will happen?

What are the key issues for you?

What do you want? What are your needs?

What are you willing to compromise on? What are you definitely not willing to compromise on?

What strategy or conflict style will you use as you approach the mediation?

Lesson 2.4E HANDOUT: MEDIATING CONFLICT ROLES

Party 1: Rachel/Richard

You are at overnight summer camp and you are having a terrible time. You can't sleep because your bunkmate reads late at night and keeps the light on. He/she also throws his/her things everywhere and you are constantly walking over his/her things. You have asked him/her to stop reading and be neater, but he/she doesn't seem to listen to your requests. You want to find a new bunkmate in a new cabin, but the camp leader has said there is nowhere to put you since no one else wants to change. The leader has suggested you speak with your camp counselor and ask him/her to help mediate the situation. You hesitantly agree.

Party 2: Natalie/Nathan

You are at overnight summer camp and you are having a terrible time. Your bunkmate is always on the phone at night and this makes it very hard for you to read, which you like to do when you're going to sleep. Also, whenever you are in the room, he/she has loud music playing that you don't like. You've asked him/her to turn it down or wear headphones, but he/she doesn't always do this. You want to find a new bunkmate in a new cabin, but the camp leader has said there is nowhere to put you since no one else wants to change. The leader has suggested you speak with your camp counselor and ask him/her to help mediate the situation. You hesitantly agree.

Party 3: Belinda/Boris the mediator

This is your third year as a camp counselor at this summer camp. You really enjoy how open and friendly everyone is. You also really like helping the campers work through their problems. You like helping them look for creative solutions when they seem blocked. You've seen a lot of conflicts at the camp over the years and you believe every conflict can have a happy ending. The camp leader has asked you to mediate a conflict between two bunkmates, both of whom want to switch to a different cabin.

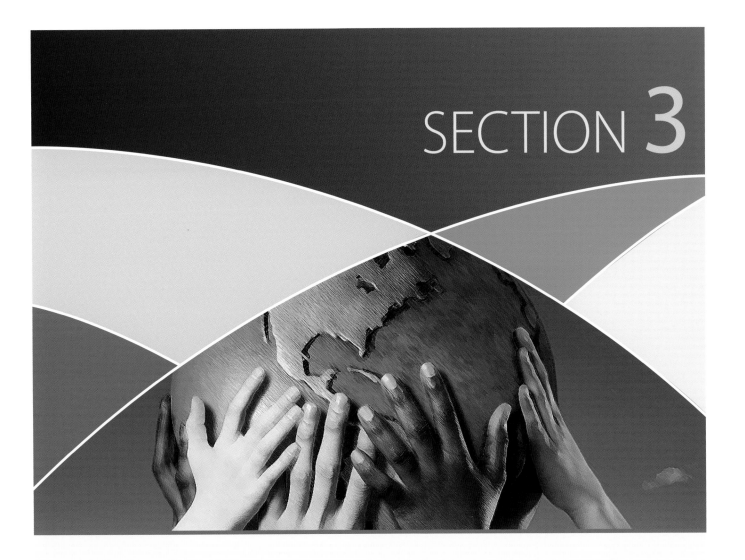

There are many ways to be a peacebuilder.

This section focuses on peacebuilders. Our goal is for students to identify with peacebuilders, recognizing that anyone can be a peacebuilder. While it is easy to view the iconic peacebuilders of our collective history as exceptional people far different from ourselves, it is important that we humanize and personalize these role models for young people to understand the characteristics and experiences that have helped these individuals promote peacebuilding so that they can recognize such qualities in themselves. It is important to point out that everyone has flaws and weaknesses and faced challenges and made mistakes, including our most famous peacebuilders. But what is important is how we overcome these challenges and continue to promote peacebuilding through our words, thoughts, and actions. Another theme of this section is that being a peacebuilder does not mean tackling huge issues right away. Building peace is something that can take place in our daily lives and in small ways; even on a personal or local level. In this section, we aim to introduce students to the range of characteristics, actions, and experiences associated with known peacebuilders, as well as organizations today that bring people together to achieve these goals on a larger scale. Whether as a student sharing ideas about peace with his or her family and peers, an educator teaching students about peacebuilding, a news reporter covering the world's conflicts, or a diplomat negotiating a peace treaty, students will learn that there are many ways to be a peacebuilder in today's society, and that they can start taking steps to build peace right now.

Preparation: If you have not done Lesson 1.2 Perspectives on Peace, you should complete that lesson with your students before beginning this section, as it invites students to create definitions of peace. If you have done that lesson, return to the definitions that students created as a way to segue into the theme that there are many ways to be a peacebuilder.

Lesson 3.1
Characteristics of Peacebuilders

Rationale

It is important for students to be able to identify with and see themselves in famous peacebuilders, as this can help demystify what it means to be a peacebuilder and can lead students to the conclusion that they too can make a difference in the world. In this activity, students begin to explore the diversity of characteristics that can be identified with peacebuilders, as well as characteristics they may share or wish to develop.

Objectives

1. To introduce students to peacebuilders and examine how they promote peace.
2. To identify characteristics of peacebuilders.

Standards

◆ Individual Development and Identity
◆ Civic Ideals and Practices

Time: One class period (45 minutes)

Materials

❏ Internet access or books on peacebuilders
❏ *What Does it Take to be a Peacebuilder?* Handout

45 minutes

Procedures

I. Essential Questions

What does it take to be a peacebuilder?

II. Motivation (5 minutes)

1. Revisit student definitions of peace from Lesson 1.2 or complete the initial exercise *When I Say Conflict, You Think of. . .* in Lesson 1.1, using the word peace instead of conflict.
2. Ask students:
   ◆ Who are the peacebuilders in our world? (past or present)
3. Write students' responses on the board. If students do not provide an international selection of peacebuilders, add some peacebuilders from around the world. See examples of Nobel Peace Prize winners here: http://nobelprize.org/nobel_prizes/peace/laureates/

III. Teacher Directed (5 minutes)

1. Divide students into pairs and have each pair select a peacebuilder they know from the list they generated.
2. Distribute the Handout *What Does it Take to Be a Peacebuilder?* and review it with students.

IV. Guided Practice/Independent Practice (25 minutes)

1. Have students complete the worksheet based on what they know.
2. Have groups share with the class and while they are sharing, write on the board the list of characteristics of a peacebuilder that they mention.
3. Lead a discussion using the following questions:
   ◆ What common characteristics do you notice among these peacebuilders?
   ◆ Did you notice differences in the characteristics of peacebuilders from the United States and peacebuilders from around the world?
   ◆ What do their stories tell you about the different ways of being a peacebuilder?
4. Have students turn to the partner they were working with and share the following:
   a. Share a characteristic you think you have that makes you an effective peacebuilder.
   b. Share a characteristic that you think you need to work on.
5. Ask a few volunteers to share their responses.

V. Discussion (10 minutes)

Lead more discussion using the following questions:

◆ How can you develop your characteristics that are not as strong?
◆ Based on these activities, what does it mean to be a peacebuilder?
◆ Can anyone be a peacebuilder? Can you choose to be a peacebuilder?
◆ Is there such a thing as an ideal peacebuilder?

Concluding teacher comments:

There are no inherent characteristics that make one a peacebuilder. We can all learn from the actions of other peacebuilders and develop the skills and knowledge to promote peacebuilding in our own way.

There is no ideal peacebuilder. We all have areas that we can work on, which provide a good set of specific goals toward which we can all work. Being a peacebuilder requires continual effort, self-improvement, and self-reflection, no matter what our age or experience.

Assessment:

Discussion, words generated

Extension Activity 1

Have students research a peacebuilder they have never heard of, using the same questions from the *What Does It Take to Be a Peacebuilder* Handout and present their findings to the class. One easy guide would be Nobel Peace Prize winners.

http://nobelprize.org/nobel_prizes/peace/laureates/

Extension Activity 2

Have students select one of the peacebuilders discussed at the beginning of class. Ask them to research that peacebuilder and identify obstacles the peacebuilder faced in promoting peace. How did they respond? What characteristics did they have that helped them overcome adversity?

Lesson 3.1 WORKSHEET: WHAT DOES IT TAKE TO BE A PEACEBUILDER?

Directions: Discuss the following questions about your peacebuilder with your partner. Take notes so that you can share with another group.

1. Who is your peacebuilder?

2. What acts did your peacebuilder perform that contributed to him/her being associated with peace?

3. What characteristics did your peacebuilder have that you think contributed to his/her success?

4. What challenges did he/she face?

Lesson 3.2
Peacebuilders in Action

Rationale

In this activity, students explore peacebuilders in action. Learning from peacebuilders from the past can provide valuable lessons about what we need to know and do to build peace in the present. Additionally, learning about peacebuilders can leave students feeling empowered to embrace the role of peacebuilder themselves.

Objectives

1. To learn about the work of peacebuilders around the world.
2. To identify lessons from the work of peacebuilders which students can apply to their own lives and efforts to build peace.

Standards

◆   Individual Development and Identity

◆   Civic Ideals and Practices

Time: One class period (45 minutes)

Materials

❏   Biography sheets about peacebuilders pulled from the Nobel Prize website
    http://nobelprize.org/nobel_prizes/peace/laureates/ or other sources

❏   *Information Gathering Sheet for Peacebuilders* Worksheet

❏   *Note-taking Sheet for Peacebuilders Exchange* Worksheet

❏   Poster board, markers, crayons, colored pencils (optional)

Preparation

Prior to class, download biographies of peacebuilders who do international work and attach an *Information Gathering Sheet for Peacebuilders* Worksheet to each biography. Try to include an international selection of peacebuilders and individuals with whom the students are not familiar, i.e., individuals they did not mention in Lesson 3.1. If you use the Nobel Peace Prize website, you can combine information from the biographies and press releases, but you may need to edit for length. If you have a media specialist, ask them to assist you in securing biographical material that suits your students' level.

In the interest of time, you may want to give biographies and note-taking sheets to students to complete for homework the night before.

45 minutes

Procedures

I. Essential Question:

What can we learn from peacebuilders?

II. Motivation (1 minute)

Tell students they are about to meet some real life peacebuilders! They are going to do this by BECOMING a famous peacebuilder.

III. Teacher Directed (2 minutes)

1. Tell students they will read biographical information about their peacebuilder, BECOME that peacebuilder, and then participate in a gathering of the International Peacebuilders Exchange, where peacebuilders get together to share their experiences and help others be more successful at building peace.
2. Tell students they will have 15 minutes to read about their peacebuilder, answer some questions about her/him, and then get into character (or they can do this for homework the night before). They will then have 20 minutes to meet other peacebuilders and take notes about what they learned about those people.

IV. Guided Practice (15 minutes)

1. Distribute a biography and attached *Information Gathering Sheet for Peacebuilders* Worksheet to each student.
2. Have students read the bio sheet they have been assigned and answer the questions on their worksheet. Keep students informed of how much time they have left to take notes about their peacebuilder.

V. Independent Practice (20 minutes)

1. After 20 minutes, hand out the *Note-taking Sheet for Peacebuilders Exchange* Worksheet.
2. Explain that they will circulate throughout the party to meet four other peacebuilders and take notes about them.
3. Begin the exchange.

VI. Discussion (7 minutes)

1. After 20 minutes, end the exchange and have all students take their seats.
2. Lead a discussion using these questions:
    ◆ Which peacebuilders had you never heard of before?
    ◆ What is one thing you learned about a peacebuilder you met at the gathering?
    ◆ What lessons can we learn from these peacebuilders that will help us build peace in our lives and in the world?
    ◆ Having learned about the characteristics and actions of international peacebuilders, can you begin to envision yourself as a peacebuilder? What would it look like if you were a peacebuilder?

Extension Activity 1

Have students create an inspirational poster about a peacebuilder. Divide students into groups of three. Have them decide on one of the peacebuilders they met at the exchange to focus on for this activity. Distribute poster board, markers, crayons, colored pencils, etc. Ask students what their peacebuilder would say to encourage others to build peace. Tell them to create an inspirational poster that shares what their peacebuilder would say. When they are done, have each group share their poster.

Extension Activity 2

To build upon the activity of becoming a famous peacebuilder, have students imagine a future where they are now famous peacebuilders. Have them write a short news article that profiles and describes who they are and what they have done in their life to be identified as a peacebuilder.

Note: If you are visiting the Global Peacebuilding Center at the United States Institute of Peace, the Witness Stations there will enable you to see some of these peacebuilders in action. Tell your class, "Let's meet some of the real people!" and watch the witness videos. If not visiting the Global Peacebuilding Center, consider watching the videos online at www.buildingpeace.org.

Lesson 3.2 WORKSHEET: INFORMATION GATHERING SHEET FOR PEACEBUILDERS

Teachers: Attach this sheet to each student's individual bio sheet.

Prepare for the Peacebuilders Exchange!!!

1. Look at the attached biographical information. Write down your NEW name from the top of the page.

   My real name is _____ , but now I am _____ .

2. Read over the bio sheet and answer the questions below. You will share the answers with other people who want to learn about you in your peacebuilder role.

   a. List three interesting facts about you.

   b. With whom did you work to build peace?

   c. What strategies did you use to build peace (listening skills, negotiation, mediation, etc.)?

   d. What kind of changes were the result of your work?

   e. What is the most important thing other people should know about you?

Lesson 3.2 WORKSHEET: NOTE-TAKING SHEET FOR PEACEBUILDERS EXCHANGE

Directions: Write at least four pieces of information about four other peacebuilders that you meet during the gathering. Take notes in the spaces below.

1. Name of the peacebuilder you met: _____

At least four things you learned about the peacebuilder:

1	
2	
3	
4	

2. Name of the peacebuilder you met _____

At least four things you learned about the peacebuilder:

1	
2	
3	
4	

3. Name of the peacebuilder you met: _____

At least four things you learned about the peacebuilder:

1	
2	
3	
4	

4. Name of the peacebuilder you met _____

At least four things you learned about the peacebuilder:

1	
2	
3	
4	

Lesson 3.3
Organizations Working for Peace

Rationale

Peacebuilding organizations can be as large as national governments or as small as a single person. In this lesson, students will explore the history, growth, and activities of a variety of organizations dedicated to promoting peacebuilding, as well as consider the potential for all types of organizations to play a positive role in peacebuilding.

Objectives

1. To identify organizations working to build peace.
2. To learn how students can contribute to the mission of some organizations.

Standards

◆ Individual Development and Identity
◆ Individuals, Groups and Institutions

Time: 1.5 class periods (70 minutes—45 minutes for preparation the first day and 25 minutes for presentations and discussion on the second day)

Materials

❑ *Note-Taking Form for Researching a Peacebuilding Organization* Worksheet
❑ *Creating a Commercial* Handout
❑ Miscellaneous art supplies that students might need for their commercials
❑ Flip Video Camera (optional)
❑ TV (optional, only necessary if you film the commercials)

Preparation

If your students do not have access to the Internet to conduct research in class, you will have to select organizations for groups to research and print information about each organization prior to class.

45 minutes

Part 1

Procedures

Extension Activity 1

Have students turn their commercial into a print advertisement or poster.

I. Essential Questions:

1. How do organizations work as peacebuilders?
2. Why are organizations important in helping individuals promote peace?

II. Motivation (5 minutes)

1. Tell students that they are going to look beyond individual peacebuilders and focus on organizations that work for peacebuilding. Ask:
    ◆ What organizations do you know of that build peace?

Extension Activity 2

Have students research an individual who works for an organization dedicated to peacebuilding. What is his/her job description? What is his/her academic and professional background? Interview this person by phone or email to learn more about what they do and why they chose to do it.

2. Write student responses on the board. If they have difficulty generating a list, you can use some of the organizations from the list of Nobel Peace Prize winners. An article listing winners (both people and organizations) appears at this link: http://nobelprize.org/nobel_prizes/peace/articles/lundestad-review/. Also, the United States Institute of Peace has a comprehensive list of international organizations at this link: http://www.usip.org/publications/international-organizations.
3. Ask students what kind of organizations they have identified: local, national, international, governmental, nonprofit? What are some of the differences between these kinds of organizations? Note that governments, themselves, can work for peace. The U.S. is often a third party engaged in building peace. Parties in conflict often look to trusted outside governments to help end conflicts in their region.

III. Teacher Directed (10 minutes)

1. Tell students that when groups work together to prevent or manage conflicts, they can sometimes reach wider audiences and get more people engaged because they have the structures in place to do so.
2. Share that in groups of three, students will research a national or an international organization that works for international peace, e.g. USIP, U.N., or Peace Links, an international women's peace education group founded in 1981, which was a major force in ending the Nuclear Arms race, and write a commercial about that organization which they will perform in front of the class. If you have a video camera, you may choose to film the performances.
3. Distribute the *Note-Taking Form for Researching a Peacebuilding Organization* Worksheet and the *Creating a Commercial About a Peacebuilding Organization* Handout. Review both with students.
4. Divide students into groups of three. Assign each student an international organization that works for peace or allow them to select their own from a list you have generated, from the list they generated at the beginning of class, or from their own research. If students do not have access to the Internet in class for researching their organization, prior to class you will need to determine the organizations to be researched and print information from each organization's website for students to review. Again, the United States Institute of Peace has a comprehensive list of international organizations at the following link: http://www.usip.org/publications/international-organizations and the Nobel Prize website has information about organizations that have won the peace prize.

IV. Guided/Independent Practice (30 minutes)

Circulate as students are researching, writing, and practicing their commercials.

 25 minutes

Part 2

Procedures

I. Independent Practice (15 minutes)

Have students present their commercials.

II. Discussion (10 minutes)

Lead a class discussion using some or all of the following questions:

◆ What similarities and differences did you notice in the organizations represented in the commercials?

◆ Which organization would you most likely support? Why? How would you want to support it?

◆ Why is it important that we work together in organized groups to build peace?

Assessment:

Note-taking forms and commercials (You can use the guidelines on the *Creating a Commercial About a Peacebuilding Organization* Handout)

Extension Activity 3

Have students think about a current conflict or social issue, whether locally, nationally, or internationally. Tell them to imagine that they are going to start their own non-profit organization. What is the organization called? What is its mission? Who will be involved? What activities will they do? Develop a logo for the organization. This could be done at home individually, or in groups in class.

Extension Activity 4

Many countries and governments play important roles in peacebuilding, the United States being one of them. Have students explore the role of the United States in negotiating peace in international conflicts (Northern Ireland, Israeli-Palestinian Territories, Balkans, etc.) What influence does the U.S. have on peace throughout the world? U.S. historical examples might include: President Theodore Roosevelt's mediation between Russia and Japan that led to the Portsmouth Treaty in 1905 (for which he won the Nobel Peace Prize), the vision of President Woodrow Wilson for a League of Nations and then the post–World War II development of international institutions such as the United Nations, the World Bank, and the World Health Organization as well as international treaties on human rights, war crimes, and nuclear non-proliferation. American peacebuilding efforts include the Marshall Plan, which was a massive effort to rebuild a devastated Europe after World War II. Less than fifteen years later, another peacebuilding effort was announced in the U.S.: the establishment of the Peace Corps, an organization that recruits volunteers who would dedicate themselves to the progress and peace of developing countries by teaching and transferring skills in needy communities around the world. And in 1984, Congress created the United States Institute of Peace.

Lesson 3.3 WORKSHEET: NOTE-TAKING FORM FOR RESEARCHING A PEACEBUILDING ORGANIZATION

Directions: Research your organization and answer the questions below. When you are finished with the questions, you can begin to create and rehearse your commercial.

What is the name of the organization? _____

Why does the organization exist? What is its mission?   How does the organization carry out its mission? What does it do?
What is the organization's target audience?
What is the history of the organization? How did it get started?
Where is the organization located and where does it do its work?
How can people get involved to support the organization (donate, volunteer, etc.)?

Handout 3.3 HANDOUT: CREATING A COMMERCIAL ABOUT A PEACEBUILDING ORGANIZATION

Directions   Use the following steps to create your commercial about a peace organization.

Step One   Select your peace organization. Write its name here.

Name: _____

Step Two   Research your organization using the internet. Take notes on the *Note-Taking Form about Peacebuilding Organizations* Worksheet. Be sure to cover all topics listed on the form.

Step Three   From your notes create a 30 second commercial about the organization, using the guidelines below. You can write the commercial in script form or you can make a story board to illustrate the commercial. To make a story board, draw a series of squares on a piece of paper and in each square show the action that is taking place in the commercial. When you look at the squares in order, you see the story that the commercial is telling.

Guidelines

- The commercial should be 30 seconds or shorter.
- The commercial should include accurate information that covers ALL of the note-taking topics.
- The commercial should include all three members of the team.
- The commercial should be creative in some way (e.g., includes a jingle, is humorous, has props, etc.)
- The commercial should engage the viewer. At the end of the commercial, the viewer should want to learn more about the organization and the work it does.

Step Four   Once the commercial is written, REHEARSE with the members of the team. Make any props necessary.

Step Five   Perform your commercial!

Lesson 3.4
Making a Difference: Becoming a Peacebuilder

Rationale

Peacebuilding is an active process. It is a combination of knowledge, skills, and intentional behaviors. Being a peacebuilder is not always easy, but having a toolkit of skills and strategies can facilitate action. This lesson asks students to identify the consequences and challenges of being a peacebuilder and strategies to overcome these challenges and promote peacebuilding on a daily basis.

Objectives

1. To identify the challenges and consequences of being a peacebuilder.
2. To consider ways to overcome these challenges.

Standards

◆ Individual Development and Identity
◆ Civic Ideals and Practices

Time: One class period (45 minutes)

Materials

❑ Banner that states: It isn't enough to talk about peace. One must believe in it. And it isn't enough to believe in it. One must work at it. —Eleanor Roosevelt (Consider having the art teacher work with students to create this)
❑ *Making a Difference: Becoming a Peacebuilder Discussion Director Card* Handout (one for each group)
❑ *Making a Difference: Becoming a Peacebuilder Note-taker's Card* Worksheet

45 minutes

Procedures

I. Essential Questions

1. How will I be a peacebuilder in daily life?
2. What steps will I take to overcome the challenges to being a peacebuilder in daily life?

II. Motivation (10 minutes)

1. Ask students:
   - What are some of the many ways you can be a peacebuilder?
2. Brainstorm with the class different conflict situations (local, national, and international) and ways they can be a peacebuilder in those situations. Remind students that there are many ways of being a peacebuilder. Examples include: using inclusive language, helping two friends see each other's point of view, and challenging assumptions.

III. Teacher Directed (10 minutes)

1. Place a banner across the board that states (or write on the board), "It isn't enough to talk about peace. One must believe in it. And it isn't enough to believe in it. One must work at it."—Eleanor Roosevelt.
2. Distribute three sticky notes to each student.
3. Direct them to write three tips for being a peacebuilder in daily life that anyone could follow.

IV. Guided Practice (7 minutes)

Call students up one at a time and have them read aloud their sticky notes as they stick them to the board underneath the banner.

V. Independent Practice (10 minutes)

1. Divide students into groups of four. Ask one member of the group to be the discussion director and one member of the team to be the note-taker.
2. Have the elected discussion directors and note-takers raise their hands and give them the *Making a Difference: Becoming a Peacebuilder Discussion Director Card* Handout and *Making a Difference: Becoming a Peacebuilder Note-taker's Card* Worksheet, respectively. Review the directions and check for understanding. Share that the groups have fifteen minutes to chat and develop a human sculpture that they will present to the class in response to the question:
   - How can you deal with the risks of being a peacebuilder?

   A human sculpture (also known as a tableau) is a frozen snapshot of something, created with bodies. It is often used to test comprehension of ideas by having small groups of students create one to summarize or capture what they just learned.

VI. Discussion (8 minutes)

1. Have each team share their human sculpture.
2. Lead a discussion using some or all of the following questions:
   ◆ What were the common themes in the sculptures?
   ◆ In what ways is building peace internationally more difficult than building peace in your own community or country? What additional challenges do you face when trying to create peace internationally?
   ◆ How can you overcome these additional challenges?
   ◆ What steps will you take as an individual to deal with the challenges you face while trying to build peace?

Assessment:

Human sculpture

Extension Activity 1

Have students research people who took risks to build peace, answering the following questions: What risks did they face? How did they overcome these challenges? You can refer your students to the witness videos on the Global Peacebuilding Center Website at www.buildingpeace.org for possible individuals to research.

Extension Activity 2

Have students create a brochure with the "Top Ten Tips for Being a Peacebuilder" that they can share with younger students in the school.

Lesson 3.4 HANDOUT: MAKING A DIFFERENCE: BECOMING A PEACEBUILDER DISCUSSION DIRECTOR CARD

Directions

Part One: Lead your group in discussing the following questions. Make sure that everyone participates and that you give your note-taker enough time to jot down notes.

- Why might it be difficult to be a peacebuilder? What keeps people from working for peace more frequently?
- What are the benefits of being a peacebuilder?
- What are some of the risks involved in being a peacebuilder in your community or internationally? How can you deal with these risks?

Part Two: When you are done with your discussion, create a human sculpture that somehow reflects a response or responses to

- How can you deal with the risks of being a peacebuilder?

Use the notes your note-taker took if necessary. Every group member must be part of the sculpture.

Lesson 3.4 WORKSHEET: MAKING A DIFFERENCE: BECOMING A PEACEBUILDER
NOTETAKER'S CARD

Directions: Take notes about each question while your group is talking.

1. Why might it be difficult to be a peacebuilder? What keeps people from working on international conflicts more frequently?

2. What are the benefits of being a peacebuilder?

3. What are some of the risks involved in being a peacebuilder in your community or internationally? How can you deal with these risks?

Lesson 3.5
Taking a Step Toward Peacebuilding

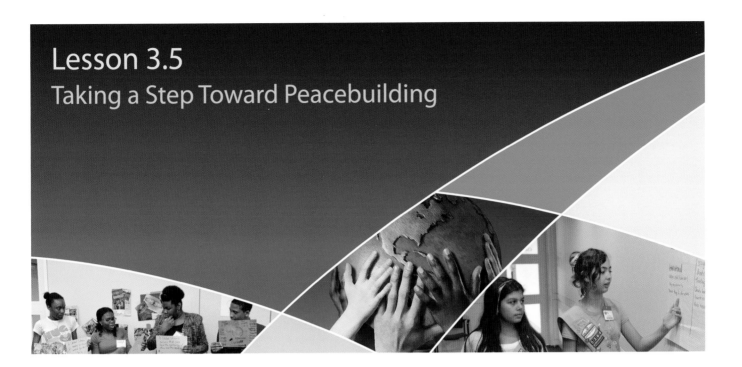

Rationale

As a peacebuilder, focusing on a large and abstract goal such as "building world peace" is far too general and unrealistic. Building peace involves concrete decisions and defined, measurable actions we take every day to promote the ideas and conditions necessary to build less violent communities. The aim of this lesson is for students to develop specific and realistic actions they can take to contribute to peacebuilding locally and globally.

Objectives

To develop realistic actions students can take to contribute to building peace.

Standards

◆ Civic Ideals and Practices

Materials

❑ Index cards
❑ 12 x 12 piece of sketch paper
❑ 12 x 12 piece of construction paper, foam board, wood, etc.
❑ Random found objects and art materials for their stepping-stones (you can ask students to bring in natural and found objects prior to the lesson).

Time: 1.5 class periods (75 minutes)

45 minutes

Part 1

Procedures

I. Essential Question

What actions can you take to build peace?

II. Motivation (10 minutes)

1. Give each student an index card and ask them to write down their response to the following questions:
   ◆ What kind of changes would you like to see in the world to make it more peaceful? What steps will you take to make this happen?
2. Ask students to share what they wrote.

III. Teacher Directed (5 minutes)

1. Tell students that now that they've talked about the changes they want to see in the world, they're going to focus on how to get there.
2. Give each student a piece of 12 × 12 paper. Share that each student will create a stepping-stone that will become a step toward peacebuilding. This piece of paper will be for sketching their stone. Later they will put their sketch on another material. Share that the focus of the stepping-stone should be steps/actions that they can take on a daily, monthly, or yearly basis to create the change they want to see in the world. To add to their stepping-stones, they can use the characteristics they generated about peacebuilders, a quote made by a peacebuilder, a peacebuilding organization they learned about, or a tip for becoming a peacebuilder—all discussed in earlier lessons.

IV. Guided Practice (20 minutes)

1. Give students time to sketch their idea.
2. Once they are done, have them share their sketch with you, and then give them the final piece of construction paper/wood/etc., to draw their sketch.

V. Independent Practice (10 minutes)

Students work on their stepping-stones.

Extension Activity 1

Work with the art teacher to turn their stepping stone creations into real stepping-stones that can be placed around the school.

Extension Activity 2

Have students develop a peacebuilder's pledge. In small groups, they develop a pledge of what actions and attitudes they pledge to uphold to actively promote peacebuilding in the world (these could be partially taken from the stepping-stones). Put the pledges up on the wall and have students work as a whole class to consolidate their pledges into one pledge statement. Have students raise their hand if they agree to all aspects of the pledge. Negotiate changes as necessary until everyone agrees. Write the pledge on large poster board and have all the students sign it. Place the pledge in a visible place in the classroom to see throughout the year. Emphasize that the class is now a community of peacebuilders, and that from here on, they all pledge to support each other in building peace.

---

 30 minutes

Part 2

Procedures

I. Independent Practice Continued (20 minutes)

Students continue to work on their stepping-stones.

II. Closure (10 minutes)

1. Lay out stepping-stones on the floor in a pathway.
2. Have students walk alongside them to see all of the stepping-stones.
3. Close by having each student share one word to describe how they feel now that they have completed several lessons on conflict management and peacebuilding.

APPENDIX

A. Participation Rubric

Standards	Does Not Meet Objective	Partially Meets Objective	Meets Objective	Exceeds Expectations
	◆ Student **seldom** takes an active role in his/her own learning. ◆ He/she **rarely** participates and asks questions infrequently. ◆ Student hesitates to share ideas or to take risks, and may not always listen to or respect the opinions of others. ◆ Student usually **participates only when called upon.** ◆ As a result of assignments being incomplete or missing, student **may not be prepared to answer thoughtfully with detail or substance.** ◆ Student needs **regular reminders to stay on task, and a meeting with the teacher** and parent(s) may be required to reestablish the expectations for participation.	◆ Student **sometimes** takes an active role in his/her learning, sharing relevant ideas, and asking appropriate questions. ◆ Although **reluctant to take risks,** student contributes regularly to class discussions. ◆ Student listens to his/her classmates and respects their opinions. ◆ As a result of having completed assignments, the student is prepared to answer questions **when called upon.** ◆ The student **may need occasional reminders to stay** on task, to make the most of class time, and to increase his/her level of commitment to the course.	◆ Student **consistently** takes an active role in own learning. ◆ Student participates regularly in class discussions and **frequently volunteers his/her ideas,** asks thoughtful questions, and defends opinions. ◆ Student **listens respectfully to classmates and is willing to share** ideas as a result of having completed assignments. ◆ Though **never causing disruption** to the class, this student **does not always demonstrate a consistent commitment** to make the most out of our class time each and every day.	◆ Student **always** takes a voluntary, thoughtful, and active role in his/her learning, **challenging himself/herself** on a daily basis. ◆ Through participation and inquiry, student consistently demonstrates a genuine desire to learn and share ideas with classmates and teacher. He/she **initiates** discussions, **asks significant questions, paraphrases others' comments when making his/her own,** and acts as a leader within the group. ◆ Student is **willing to take risks,** assert an opinion and support it, and listen actively to others. ◆ Student is always **well prepared** to contribute to the class as a result of having thoughtfully completed assignments, and the thoroughness of his/her work demonstrates the high regard he/she holds for learning.
Points	1	2	3	4
Grade Equivalent	D	C	B	A

B. Peacebuilding Toolkit for Educators Feedback Form

Directions: The *Peacebuilding Toolkit for Educators* is intended to be a living document: your experience using the lessons with your students and the feedback you provide us will enable us to continually develop and improve this resource. Please take a few moments to share your thoughts below and mail this feedback form to United States Institute of Peace, Global Peacebuilding Center, 2301 Constitution Avenue, NW, Washington, DC 20037. Alternatively, you can complete a feedback form online at www.buildingpeace.org.

Please note: This form is anonymous. However, if you would be willing to communicate with Education staff about your feedback, please include your e-mail address here:

_____

Grades in which you used the Toolkit lessons: _____

Subjects in which you used the Toolkit lessons: _____

How did you hear about the Toolkit? _____

1. On a scale of 1 to 10 (with 1 being the lowest and 10 being the highest), please circle the number which indicates how you rate the *Peacebuilding Toolkit for Educators* overall as a supplement to your curriculum.

    1   2   3   4   5   6   7   8   9   10

2. On a scale of 1 to 10 (with 1 being the lowest and 10 being the highest), please circle the number which indicates how engaging the lessons were for your students.

    1   2   3   4   5   6   7   8   9   10

3. On a scale of 1 to 10 (with 1 being the lowest and 10 being the highest), please circle the number below which indicates how easily you were able to connect the lessons to your content standards.

    1   2   3   4   5   6   7   8   9   10

4. On a scale of 1 to 10 (with 1 being the lowest and 10 being the highest), please circle the number that indicates how easy the lesson format was to use.

    1   2   3   4   5   6   7   8   9   10

5. On a scale of 1 to 10 (with 1 being the lowest and 10 being the highest), please circle the number which indicates how likely you are to share the *Peacebuilding Toolkit for Educators* with your colleagues.

    1   2   3   4   5   6   7   8   9   10

6. Which lessons did you find most effective in terms of content or methods? Why?

7. Which lessons did you find least effective in terms of content or methods? Why?

8. What modifications did you make to any of the lessons, which you think should be incorporated in future editions of the *Peacebuilding Toolkit for Educators*?

9. What additional content do you think should be added to the *Peacebuilding Toolkit for Educators*?

10. What additional content/resources for students and educators did you access at www.buildingpeace.org to supplement the lessons?

11. Please share concrete examples of how your students benefited from or were impacted by the content and lessons in the *Peacebuilding Toolkit for Educators* (continue on another sheet, as needed).

About the Editor

Alison Milofsky is a senior program officer at the United States Institute of Peace specializing in teacher education and curriculum development at the secondary level. She works with educators domestically and in conflict zones to integrate conflict management concepts into the curriculum. Additionally, she teaches courses on facilitation and dialogue in the Institute's Academy for International Conflict Management and Peacebuilding and trains international police and UN Peacekeepers in communication and negotiation skills. Milofsky has facilitated education and training programs in the Middle East, Africa, Southeast Asia, and Central Asia. She currently teaches dialogue courses on race and gender for undergraduate students at the University of Maryland. Milofsky holds a BA from McGill University and a PhD in education policy, with a specialization in curriculum theory and development, from the University of Maryland.

About the Contributors

Kristina Berdan is a teacher in Baltimore City Schools. She graduated from Towson University's master of arts in teaching program after earning her BS in Criminal Justice at the University of Maryland. She is currently the Teacher-Director of The Youth Dreamers, Inc., a nonprofit organization created by her students in 2001 to decrease violence among youth after school through the creation of a youth-run youth center. She was on the editorial team to produce *Writing for a Change: Boosting Literacy and Learning through Social Action*, Jossey-Bass, 2006. She earned her National Board Certification in 2000, received the B-More Fund Award in November 2006, and was an Open Society Institute Community Fellow in 2007. She teaches in the Teaching Artist Institute with Young Audiences of Maryland and with Towson University's Arts Integration Institute. She is a part-time faculty member in the Maryland Institute College of Art MA in Community Arts Program.

Sarah Bever is the education program manager at Mercy Corps Action Center to End World Hunger in New York City. She also works as a teaching artist and professional development coordinator for the International Theater and Literacy Project in Arusha, Tanzania. Prior to moving to New York, she was a theater teacher at Herndon High School in Fairfax County. She has an MA in international education development with a concentration in peace education and curriculum from Teachers College, Columbia University where she was the co-director of the Global Initiative for Social Change and the Arts.

Danielle Goldberg is a diversity training specialist and mediator with more than eight years experience managing international and domestic education programs, including the Anti-Defamation League's A WORLD OF DIFFERENCE® Institute and Echoes & Reflections: A Multi-Media Curriculum on the Holocaust. From 2009–2010, Danielle was an Atlas Corps fellow in Bogotá, Colombia working with the NGO Give to Colombia to channel international resources and building public-private alliances in support of innovative social development projects throughout Colombia. During that time, she also presented at the 2010 International Institute on Peace Education in Cartagena, Colombia. In addition to working with Voices for Sudan, a coalition of US-based organizations in the Diaspora devoted to promoting peace and development in Sudan, she is currently Program Coordinator for Columbia University's Institute for the Study of Human Rights coordinating a Peacebuilding Development

Initiative in Darfur. Goldberg possesses an MA in international peace and conflict resolution from American University.

Nora Gordon has been studying and practicing conflict resolution for a decade. She is the assistant to the ambassador from Afghanistan to the United Nations. Nora holds a master's in international affairs with a focus on conflict resolution from Columbia University's School of International and Public Affairs. She majored in peace and conflict Studies at UC Berkeley and has worked on peacebuilding projects in Timor-Leste, Liberia, Rwanda, Brazil, the West Bank, Syria, the Brazilian Amazon, and New York. In Rwanda she assisted with leadership trainings and helped facilitate dialogue for high-level government and NGO leaders. Through the Women's Refugee Commission, Nora designed facilitation tools in Liberia for job training programs. Nora spent three years coordinating programs for the peace education organization, Brooklyn For Peace. She spent summer 2009 researching in Timor-Leste with Columbia's Center for International Conflict Resolution. With the U.S.-Syria Grassroots Diplomacy Program, she co-facilitated conflict resolution workshops in Syria.

Illana Lancaster is an assistant professor in the international training and education program in the School of Education, Training, and Health at American University in Washington, DC. As a Peace Corps Volunteer, she taught English in a community junior secondary school in Botswana. Her teaching career includes instructing at Bell Multicultural High School (now Columbia Heights Education Center), Koc University in Istanbul, Montgomery College in Maryland, and the University of Maryland. She also has worked as a curriculum specialist focusing on curricula development for English language learners. Lancaster holds a BA from the University of Virginia, an M.Ed. from The George Washington University, and a PhD in international education policy from the University of Maryland. Her current research interests include gender, urban education, critical race theory, and social-spatial analysis.

In her sixth year of teaching seventh grade social studies and eighth grade ethics at Green Acres School, **Adriana Murphy** completed her master's degree in Private School Leadership from Columbia University Teachers College. She is dean of the 7/8 Unit and director of service learning. She earned a bachelor's degree in history from Bishop's University in Quebec and a master's degree in peace, development, and international conflict management at the Universitat Jaume I in Spain. A strong proponent of children's ethical development, she published two books in two years: *Highly Effective Character Education Programs in Independent Schools* and *Twenty-One for Teens, Case Studies for Students in Grades 7–12*. Prior to teaching, Murphy observed elections in El Salvador and Serbia. She also served in the AmeriCorps National Civilian Community Corps as a Team Leader.

A native of Michigan, **Terese Trebilcock** received her bachelor's degree in political science, economics minor, from the University of Michigan, and her master of public policy, international emphasis, also from the University of Michigan. She has worked as project manager for the Institute of Social Research, as an Intelligence Officer (political-economic analyst on Latin America) for the Central Intelligence Agency, and, for the past fourteen years, as a high school social studies teacher in Baltimore County, Maryland. She sponsors the History Club and the Hereford Philosophical Society. She has been lucky enough to have lived overseas, and continues to enjoy traveling, reading, needlework, and her family. She has been married to her husband, Craig, an immigration attorney and colonel in the Army's JAG Corps, for twenty-seven years, and is devoted to her sons, Aubrey, a junior at the University of Wisconsin, and Joseph, a freshman at Indiana University of Pennsylvania.